Chasms And Bridges
Within The Heart

By
Amanda Perry

Published by True Beginnings Publishing
Copyright 2015 by Amanda Perry

Chasms And Bridges Within The Heart, by Amanda Perry © Copyright 2015. All Rights Reserved and Preserved. No part of this book may be reproduced or transmitted in any form or by any means, electronic or mechanical, including photocopying, recording, or by information storage and retrieval systems or other electronic or mechanical methods, without written permission of the Author with exceptions as to brief quotes, references, articles, reviews and certain other noncommercial uses permitted by copyright law. For permission requests, write to the Publisher, addressed: "Attention: Permissions," at the address below.

true_beginnings_publishing@yahoo.com

Formatting, Cover Art, and Interior Graphics by True Beginnings Publishing. All Illustrations, Cover Art, and Text are Copyright Protected by: My Original Works. Reference #82642.

Ordering Information:
To order additional copies of this book, visit Amazon or please visit: https://www.createspace.com/5524566

ISBN-10: 0692458751
ISBN-13: 978-0692458754

Chasms And Bridges Within The Heart
© Amanda Perry
First Printing, 2015

Table of Contents

The Temptation Of A Bulimic	1
A Walk Through The Garden	3
Stolen Innocence	8
Voice	11
Sun	13
My Grandma	14
I Am Here	16
Abduction	19
Chosen Obedience	23
Found In The Eyes Of Serenity	27
Life Changing Reflections	30
Glory	32
Dying In Love	35
Secret Friend	39
Comfort On A Cloud	42
Feeding The Flame Of The Fire	46
The Dragon's Lair	51
Essence Of Writing	57
Heavenly Gift	58
Reflective Deception	59

Temptation	61
The Blessed Hope	64
Wonderfully Made	71
Beautiful Elation	73
Spring	75
Lineage Of Grace	77
Motherly Love	84
Martyrs	86
Ode To Rickie	88
Expressions Of Love	90
The Answer That Can Only Be Found In Scripture	92
Interacting With The Author	97
The First Blush Of Spring	100
The Empty Tomb	102
Control	107
The Beauty Of A Mother's Expecting	110
Exaltations From My Soul	112
Violent Forcing From Childhood	115
A Remembered Place	120
Angel Of Light	124
The Mark	131

Come To Me	135
The American Spirit	137
My Dear Serenity	139
The Creation, The Curse, And The Promise	141
Creation In The Garden Of Eden	144
Kenneth	153
For You My God	156
The Triumphal Entry	159
The Den Of Thieves	162
Through This	167
Atonement	169
Coming To A Theater Near You	185
A Memory Of A Grandpa	187
Psalm Of The King Of Glory	192
Whom Shall I Send?	196
A Wedding Eternal	203
If The Lord Is With Us, Who Can Come Against Us?	207
Nothing That We Can't Handle	211
At The Foot Of The Cross	212
Admirable Devotion	215

Dedication

To all of those in this world who feel as if they've lost themselves or their reputation forever. God can transform burnt ashes into wondrous forms of dazzling beauty.

Writing:

For as long as I can remember, I have always loved writing. I have never gotten enough of reading books, either. Some may call me a nerd or a dork or a bookworm, but it's something that I love to do.

When I write, I write about what's on my heart at the time... sometimes, my writings are memories of my past. Sometimes, it's what God had laid on my heart to share. And then, other times it's just some things that I've been through that I believe other people are or can be suffering from also.

I do not write to try to please other people. What I write, if taken the wrong way, I had no intention of writing it that way. Writing is a form of release for me... therapy, I guess some could say. I know there are people out there who like it, and people who don't, and people who could care less.

It's me... it's a part of me... take it or leave it.

Millions of people suffer every day from abuse, from eating disorders, from self infliction, from everything that I write about... maybe, they have no one to turn to... maybe, they're too scared to come forward with what they're going through... maybe, by reading some of my writings, I can help them. Reach them. Give them hope.

That's why I write...

God gave me a voice...

God gave me a life with difficult obstacles to overcome and make it through...

God gave me a talent... It's time for me to use it, no matter how ugly the truth really is or can be.

Chasms And Bridges Within The Heart

The Temptation Of A Bulimic

She remains strong and holds steadfast to her faith.
She listens to the Lord, her Father, every moment of every day.
But in the stillness of night, Satan comes along and tells her the promises of God will always break.
Go ahead and binge on food. It's simple to be beautiful, just throw what you eat up and away.
She cries in the night and falls to her knees beside her bed to pray.
Out of the darkness comes a much louder voice, more gentle and true:
It is written, that man shall not live by bread alone, but by every word of God.

You are not worthy to be God's child. You've already destroyed your body; His holy temple, you see.
Turn away from Him, and I will make your dreams come true; come worship your illness, which is indeed from me…
She closes her eyes and sees this verse in her tormented mind:
Get thee behind me, Satan: for it is written, Thou shalt worship the Lord thy God, and Him only shalt thou serve.

Amanda Perry

But is your life worth it? Comes the fierce whisper in her ear.
You will never overcome this. I will always fill you with doubt and fear.
You will never win, you see. Keep slowly killing yourself and beautiful indeed you will be.
Lord Jesus, please be with me, she silently cries.
Once more, she hears the gentle voice: It is said, Thou shalt not tempt the Lord thy God.

As the tears are silently swept away from her eyes,
Then comes a peace and comfort over her body and soul.
Praise be to Jesus! My whole being He does console!
At the last words of Jesus, she felt Satan and his power leave.
The temptation is over: God's promise of healing, love, and an eternal home she proudly and willingly does receive.

Chasms And Bridges Within The Heart

A Walk Through The Garden

Come with me and please take my hand; it's a beautiful evening for a walk through the garden with me.
The skies are clear and millions of stars are shining their light.
Let the pale moonlight be our guide; let us move forward and see in the garden what beauty there may be.
Leaves of the many trees are quivering in the light whispers of the wind.
Moonlight sparkles off refreshing drops of simmering dew.
A babbling brook can be heard; singing nature a lullaby just up ahead around the bend.
Take a moment to inhale the many fragrances around you-
They fill your soul with sweet delight and comfort uneasy thoughts.
Breathing them all in; together you can feel your soul renew.

There's a gentle white mist slowly swirling around your feet.
Something in the atmosphere has begun to alert all the senses.
Blood rushes through your veins, making a daring dance together with your rapid heartbeat.
As we walk onward through the now-enveloping mists,
We come to a place most sacred and silent.
It seems as if, here, the outside world no longer exists.

Amanda Perry

Draw in your breath and hold it; try not to make a sound.
Afraid the vision you're seeing will disappear with a blink of an eye,
Appears a most beautiful man silently kneeling onto His knees upon the cool, hard ground.
Behold a sight most wondrous to see;
His face is gazing up toward the heavens; eyes closed and lips moving in the most silent and fervent fashion.
Something about this man seems to reach out and comfort you;
A warm sensation flows over your skin, and your soul is no longer burdened but feels completely set free.
Pools of moonlight beams all around Him, erasing the shadows of the night,
Soaking His whole body in a beautiful pale glow.
What a privilege! What a delight! To be one of two people in this garden to stumble upon this most sacred site.

Eyes the color of crystal blue gaze upward toward the endless sky.
Slight trembles begin to attack His perfect body;
Tears can be seen forming in His eyes, and choking back a sob, He suddenly freely cries.
Down from off His knees, He quickly falls; placing His tearstained face upon the cool ground,
His whole body shutters in extreme convulsions.
In the garden surrounding Him, everything is still, and there appears a tremendous silence bearing all around.

Chasms And Bridges Within The Heart

The air around the garden is sweet and very cool,
Yet, He appears to be sweating profusely.
He seems to be in severe pain; fighting within His body a major duel.
Suddenly, His drops of sweat miraculously turn a most bitter color of red,
Streaming down His troubled face onto garments quickly stained.
Just to see this man suffering like this, sweating blood and shaking uncontrollably, makes me wish I could lift His burden from His head.

"Hear me, Father."
"Rise up, defend me."
"Save me from the traps they set for me."
Suddenly, silence… the atmosphere becomes thick with electrical static.
The feelings of freedom and comfort are replaced by feelings of severe doubt and endless fear.
Laughter from another man, most sinister, fills the garden with glee, most ecstatic.
A figure appears standing beside the tormented man;
Robes of the blackest black envelop him and makes him more pale.
His voice comes out smooth and silvery; his thoughts are extremely dangerous, and he will destroy you if he can.
"Do you really believe…"
"…That one man can bear…"
"…The full burden of sin?"

Amanda Perry

The trembling man lifts up His head and gazes to the sky.
His face has become bloodstained and dirty.
Severely shaking, He feels the pure power of evil surround Him and suddenly begins to cry.
"Shelter me, O Lord."
"I trust in You."
"In You I take refuge."
Both of the men gaze up at the moon as a cloud passes over it, diminishing its light.
One man a picture of endless beauty; the other an image of horrifying fright.
"No one man can carry this burden…"
"…I tell You…"
"It is far too heavy."
"Saving their souls is way too costly."
"No one. Ever."
"No."
"Never."

The man of beauty, now soaked and covered in His own sweat and blood,
Closed His eyes and began to pray…
"Father, You can do all things."
"If it is possible, let this chalice pass from Me."
"But let Your will be done…"
"…not Mine."

Chasms And Bridges Within The Heart

A great darkness fell over the entire garden, and nothing was left to see.
The sound of the body belonging to the man of beauty was heard
falling and resting on the ground.
On the other's pale face, a brilliant glowing smile came to be.
"Who is Your Father?"
"Who are You?"
The man of beauty lay silent upon the ground of this earth.
The man of horrifying fright smiled and stared as maggots crawled
between his teeth.
He gazed at the ground, and suddenly, a deadly snake from the dirt he
seemed to unearth.
As the snake slithered toward the man of beauty,
He seemed to somehow gain more strength.
Standing up, He gazed into the eyes of the man of fright,
Took his foot and slammed it down on the snake's head; killing it
became His duty.
Terrible screams and hissing came from pale, parted lips.
He glared up toward the sky, and the black cloak upon his pale body
suddenly fell to the ground.
All that was left of the man of fright were his ashes because it seems he
was burnt into a crisp.
The man of beauty slowly turned around.
He waited for the kiss of betrayal, patiently and steadfastly;
Here, in the Garden of Gethsemane, Jesus the Christ's purpose was
delivered and found.

Amanda Perry

Stolen Innocence

Filled with insufferable and ecstatic glee,
She finds herself smiling, for tomorrow is her birthday.
She is now to be considered a woman; after all, she is going on sixteen.
Away from the nightmare called her childhood, she'd flee…
Away from the nightmare called her childhood, she'd flee…

Drifting into peaceful slumber,
Something in her countenance awakes as the door opens, then closes and locks.
Before her stands her step-dad, so she begins to question,
But up onto her bed does continue to slither.
He presses his face to hers and silently mocks.
Away from the nightmare called her childhood, she'd soon flee…
Away from the nightmare called her childhood, she'd soon flee…

"Came to give you your present early," he fiercely whispers in her ear.
His calloused hands did begin to rip away the only shroud of protection.
Fear overcomes her and, silently there, she remains as her eyes do begin to tear.
Using roughness and savage strength in two hands, her body violently convulses as his hands find each section.
Away from the nightmare called her childhood, she'd soon flee…
Away from the nightmare called her childhood, she'd soon flee…

Chasms And Bridges Within The Heart

Trying desperately to fight him off was exhausting her; she was fighting a losing battle.
It hit her then as continuous movements began developing.
Searing and burning currents began cutting into her body, down to her very soul it continues this journey to rattle.
Fearing, panicking, and surviving are the only thoughts she has running through her head; why are the sounds into the background fading? Why is disturbing darkness now so suddenly enveloping?
Away from the nightmare she's now calling her childhood, she quickly begins fleeing…
Away from the nightmare she's now calling her childhood, she quickly begins fleeing…

How much time is passing, she wonders as life begins to hit her again, and slowly, she's opening her eyes.
He's standing at the door again,
And at the edges of his mouth there begins a most hateful and disgusting sneer.
"Tell anyone and mommy will be hurting." She feels her body tightly squeezing as seeping into her very soul came fear,
And extremely quickly, it started to steer.
Door opening and closing, she exhales a breath long held and turns her eyes toward the skies.
Away from this nightmare she's now calling her adulthood, she's miraculously fleeing…
Away from this nightmare she's now calling her adulthood, she's miraculously fleeing…

Amanda Perry

The news starts hitting that they're divorcing; years upon years start their journey through time.
She's became a full-grown woman, and looking through her eyes, you begin to see more wisdom,
Always reading the Bible and silently praying.
Every day has given her whole being a light,
And through her, it's always now to shine,
She has been saved and diligently prays every day
That she will one day come into Your Kingdom.
Away from the nightmare of her past, she decides to surrender and sends all of her nightmares and sins to fleeing…
Away from the nightmare of her past, she decides to surrender and sends all of her nightmares and sins to fleeing…

She willingly and thankfully receives God's gift
Of healing and continuous grace and love.
From her, the step-dad in her life had stolen innocence,
But she was given love unconditional from her true Father from up above…

Chasms And Bridges Within The Heart

Voice

Listen; open sealed ears and listen.
Can you hear the calling? It's in the whispers of the wind; please, I beg you, please surrender all doubts and suspicions...
Take a look around you and open tightly-closed eyes.
What are you seeing? A world full of chaos; listen to my words, they should come as no surprise...
A young woman lays shaking and weeping all throughout the night.
Battered and broken, tormented and severely torn; against her rapist she lost the fight.
A young child maybe three or four lays still, cold, and silent upon a bloodstained floor.
For no reason at all, someone he trusted chose to take his life; the murderer is found "not guilty" and enjoys happiness galore.
People in authority are taking things way too far and unleashing uncivilized power.
To see white law enforcers beating, mocking, and killing black innocents leaves a taste in your mouth most sour.
On the radio, on the television, and even on the phone comes reports of hatred.
Hell has opened up its monstrous gates upon the whole world; determined to destroy and conquer a religion most sacred.

Amanda Perry

What has happened to our own country of freedom and goodwill?
I can tell you, my friends. Satan is here and here to destroy and to kill.
Any person that believes in Christ Jesus and God the Father his enemy is to be.
Think back to the days of Hitler; concentration camps, unknown forms of torture, and human degradation… that was nothing compared to what you and I are about to see.
A different religion is quickly uprising, and our own country being taken over by it.
Training camps of terrorism are its main mission; complete annihilation is coming to those who refuse to this group to commit.
War? Yes, war is starting its ceaseless raging.
Please don't ignore me when I say the times are quickly changing…
This has been laid upon my heart, and the burden of it grows as each day passes immensely strong.
God has forgiven me and has given me a great voice; I now realize that I have been too shy and quiet for far too long…

Sun

My body awakens at the warmth of your caress.
My soul has been revived, and to remain joyous is now effortless.
Precious tinkles of children's laughter can be heard throughout all your rays.
An uplifting spirit in my body peacefully and happily now lays.
The world is continuously turning, waiting on your awakening kiss.
To stand in your brilliant and dazzling light surrounds my entire being with ecstatic bliss.
Drops of dew melt into sparkling diamonds in the wake of your presence.
To make everything new and reborn is your mission in life; your whole being of essence.
Electric pulses of radiating warmth descending upon;
The universe has now begun.
Good morning world; good morning sun.

Amanda Perry

My Grandma

She's in possession of a heart made entirely of gold.
She shares with all her loved ones the gifts of undying love, endless compassion, and a great passion for life; gifts that can never be bought nor sold.
Full of hardships, her life has always been.
God has stood by her side through it all, enabling her over life's obstacles to always conquer and to always win.
Upon her beautiful face, a permanent smile God has placed.
A drop, a trickle, from the Fountain of Youth it seems as if she has had a taste…
At your weakest moment, she's there right along with you,
Holding your hand and guiding you through.
She stands steadfastly erected and remains strong in the midst of troubled waters.
No matter what this life brings, her faith never falters.
She's in possession of two big, beautiful, and bright blue eyes.
The windows to her soul; a gentle spirit within her being currently lies.
A blazing and burning light surrounds her whole entire being.
When around her, the darkness of life is impossible to be found; it's as if her burning light sends it to fleeing.
One of God's own guardian angels walking among us here on earth in human disguise.
What great beauty within her precious soul lies!
Her developing and growing family is her pride and joy.

Chasms And Bridges Within The Heart

Her light and love showers all those around her when she's with her great grand-babies; her face lights up like a child's on Christmas when he opens from Santa Claus a brand new toy.
Considerate of others, she always puts their needs first.
If you're down and depressed and surrounded by endless clouds, along the way she appears like the sun and through the clouds she does burst.
My life she has definitely prospered and blessed;
I cannot imagine my life without her, I must honestly confess.
Always there for me during my darkest hour,
God has blessed her with His amazing grace and His most awesome power.
Always showering me with streams of endless love,
I have always thought of her as my other mommy; a precious and divinely appointed gift from God the Father from up above.
In her eyes reflecting back at me is wondrous wisdom, everlasting love, and strongly developed strength.
To help those who need encouragement, she will go to any length.
She accepts me just as I am,
She guides me along life's difficult path by providing me this to hold: her hand.
One of a kind, she truly is.
God has continued to bless her by giving her another year to blossom and live!

Happy Birthday to my grandma: Lytia Lee Perry.
May this coming year for you be joyous and very merry!
I love you with all of my heart,
Amanda Perry

Amanda Perry

I Am Here

Lord, my God, I'm crying out to You now.
The demons of my past are chasing me down, so humbly to my knees I bow.
Terrors of the night are surrounding me; Lord, I'm begging for Your protection somehow…

"I am here… just close your eyes…"
"I am here… listen with your soul…"
"I am here… feel as all of your fear and pain within you slowly dies…"
"I am here… listen with your soul…"

Lord, my God, please take my trembling hand.
I need comfort and acceptance from someone who truly understands.
Lift me up from Satan's severe grasp, and onto Your Holy Rock, steadfastly I will stand…

"I am here…just keep your faith…"
"I am here…don't you shed anymore tears…"
"I am here…fall into My open embrace…"
"I am here…don't you shed anymore tears…"

Chasms And Bridges Within The Heart

Lord, my God, my soul is bare and open to You.
Forgive me now for being weak and abused.
I need You now; I need Your undying love and showers of mercy,
cleansing me and making me new.

"I am here… just give Me your all…"
"I am here… run into My open arms, and I promise I will never let you fall…"
"I am here… hold your head up and stand tall…"
"I am here… run into My open arms, and I promise I will never let you fall…"

Lord, my God, I'm singing out to You.
Clouds of glory and showers of grace rain down upon me, and all of my demons You have conquered and slew.
Happiness surrounding me from all four sides; I fall to my knees again and sing honour, thanks, and my praises to You.

"I am here… come and walk with Me…"
"I am here… when life knocks you down, just call on My Name and always believe…"
"I am here… just open your eyes and standing right beside you, it's Me you will see…"
"I am here… when life knocks you down, just call on My Name and always believe…"

Amanda Perry

Lord, I thank You for reaching me.
Thank You for Your forgiveness and undying love.
Thank You for Your devotion and making me truly see.
That evil will never win, that the defeating power is sent from Heaven above.

Lord, my God, I want to thank You for reaching me.
Your clouds of glory and Your showers of grace
Are swirling all around me, saturating my entire body and face.
Thank You, Lord, for taking all of my pain and fears away.
Thank You, Lord, for Jesus's Blood that all of my sins did erase.
Thank You, Lord, for being my Father and for blessing my life for now and always…
Thank You, Lord.
Thank You, Lord.

Abduction

Some eight years or so ago, there were two sisters who were enjoying a night of fun.
They went to see a famous singing duo at a club that was in the city downtown.
The singing duo was in person absolutely amazing to see but, when they left the club, that was when their worst nightmare had begun.
They had to walk two blocks to make it to the car; waiting until a man stopped and waved them across the street with a sneering frown.
As they passed the last building, the man's car came back into sight.
Out of the darkness appeared a most menacing figure who suddenly grabbed the younger sister, pointing a gun toward the back of her head.
The older sister gasped aloud, and the man let the younger sister go and grabbed her instead; gripping both her arms in a hold that was way too tight.
She tried to scream, tried to fight, tried to escape, but the man was just so insanely strong; throwing her into his car like she was a loaf of bread.
The doors were all locked and the windows sealed as in the driver's seat sat down the man.
The two sisters gazed at one another through the thick glass of the windshield.
The younger sister mouthed the word "sorry" and turning around back down the street, she swiftly ran.
The car started moving and filling the older sister came great fear and

severe panic... Was this to be her fate? Had her death certificate been secretly sealed?

Driving down streets unknown to her, the man easily bellows his demands.

"Take your boots and pants off first..." Shaking so badly that she could not accomplish his demand, he violently reached over and down and pushed her pants to her feet.

Crying uncontrollably, she remembers her cellphone. And hiding it between the door and her seat, she quickly dialed 911. And barely finding her voice, she issues her commands.

"Where are you taking me? Are you going to kill me?" ...at the sound of her words, he reaches over and violently pulls her hair and neck to him; he could not be fooled- he had seen the light from the phone and silently reaching it to him, she admitted great defeat.

She felt herself being pushed back into her seat.

She closed her eyes tightly as a cold hand forced between her legs and groped her privately and violently.

"Please... don't kill me; I'll do whatever you want..." she kept hearing these words as in her mind they did repeat.

She listened as he moaned as his one hand continued exploring; overcome with weakness and undying fear, she began to pray to God very silently.

"Lord, give me the strength and knowledge to make it through this night alive."

Up ahead, like a beacon flashing to her was a stop sign.

She felt in the darkness and found the car's push lock, and as the car slightly slowed, she pulled up the lock and counted to five.

On five, she pulled the handle and quickly jumped out; developing strength and endurance from a Higher Power most divine.

Tucking her chin down towards her chest, she took the whole collision with the asphalt on mostly her whole right side.

When her body ceased its rolling, she could see the man's car backing up toward her in a speeding reverse.

Chasms And Bridges Within The Heart

Turning and running, running, running, she must find a place to hide. Running away from the road and onto railroad tracks, she flew; lost and losing breath and hope she stopped as suddenly her dinner came back up, being suddenly dispersed.

Drenching with sweat in the middle of winter, she falls to the ground and releases all of her emotions to run free.

Pain... severe pain... came crashing down upon her, making her vision blurry and dark.

Across the street in front of her was an apartment duplex, and on its porch sat a man; gaining courage by thinking of her younger sister, she leans against a tree.

"Do you have a phone?" She continues her screams across the street, "Please, call the police!" ...the man hung up his phone and motioned for her to walk over; he went inside and came back out with blankets, sitting one down on the concrete step, and reaching out to help her, she sat down on the soft and warm mark.

She raised up her head as the sound of a car's engine slowly in front of her came to a stop.

Her heartbeat stopped and restarted as she realized her younger sister was looking at her through the window of the cruiser's back seat.

Walking to her now and assisting her to her feet, using words most kind and gentle, was a man in uniform, a policeman, a cop.

Opening up the door, the sisters compassionately embrace and show each other waves of endless love; for they both know it was their love for one another and God's amazing grace that they did not ever, even once relent into defeat...

Amanda Perry

I wrote this after my sister and I had a gun held to our heads and was forced into an unknown man's car... he let my sister go but threw me into the car and drove off... my sister did not leave me willingly... she ran to get help. After driving for what seemed to me hours, I was ordered to remove clothes, and he groped and fondled me... Thinking I was soon going to die, I began praying to God and saw a stop sign up ahead. And I listened to God's words in my ears and jumped out and ran... by the grace of God am I and my sister still alive today... thank you Lord. I pray that someone reading this can find comfort and deliverance in the words that I write. You are not alone... someone out there understands what you've been through or are going through right now.

Chasms And Bridges Within The Heart

Chosen Obedience

Surrounded by stillness and full of disappointment that left in her mouth a taste most bitter,
She placed her beautiful head down on her arms and buried her face; this raging battle in her soul to God she began to surrender...
Her whole life, all she ever wanted was to be close to the Lord.
Like a man lost in the desert without water to quench his thirst, her heart was yearning for Him, searing her soul with pain as from a sword.
She wished she could have been among the people delivered from Egypt as her burden became more leaden.
How wonderfully blessed they'd been to see God's miracles, to walk with Moses and hear the law for the first time, to see springing from a rock sustaining water, and to taste the fulfilling manna from Heaven.
Her deep thirst for the Lord frustrated her; maybe, it was her youth that made her now feel so restless?
How could she love the Lord her God with all her heart, mind, soul, and strength if she was to be given to a man? How could she love her God fully and still give honour to a husband? The battle within her was endless.
And yet, she seemed to understand the practicality of marriage; women were vulnerable.
Roman soldiers came to her village, taking young women and leaving them abused and ruined; life was unbearable for an unprotected woman and her future always discernible.
Pax Romana promised peace to Israel; their hearts it said was going to

console.

Wouldn't it be wiser to remain unwed, rather than marry and bring children into such a world, for her and her people still fought the Roman control?

Hebrews fanning their hatred into violence, nursing their grievances, and fighting Hellenistic influences with all their being;

Others turned traitor, rejecting the God of Abraham, Isaac, and Jacob; bringing children into this world wasn't wise for all this hatred their eyes would be seeing.

Where was God in all of this? She knew He was as powerful now as He had been when the world was created.

She knew the history of her people; why must Israel repeat the cycles of disobedience, generation after generation?

For as long as she could remember, she had heard her people crying out for rescue.

Someday, the Lord would send the Deliverer; the one who would make all things right, all things new.

The Messiah. Every day she prayed for Him to come.

Her skin began to tingle and her hair prickled as she raised her head and saw a man standing before her; heart thumping with terror, she squinted at him, for he was as bright as the sun.

"Hail, thou that art highly favoured, the Lord is with thee: blessed art thou among women."

Trembling, she sat silent and shut her eyes tightly and opened them again; he was still standing there, gazing at her with kind patience as she wondered at his words and their intention.

What did his greeting mean? Were not all God's chosen people favoured? Why did he say the Lord was with her? Was he possibly the Lord?

Fear filled her, and she closed her eyes again; surely anyone who looked upon the Lord would die. She wanted another look but was it something she could afford?

"Fear not, Mary: for thou hast found favour with God."

Chasms And Bridges Within The Heart

A sob welled up inside her throat, catching her way off guard.
She wanted nothing more than to please the Lord; her head, she slowly gave a nod.
Remembering that only the moment before, she had resisted the idea of marrying Joseph, though he loved God as much as she, she blushed.
The stranger drew closer, his head inclined toward her; he said precious words that filled her with joy and happiness in her veins rapidly rushed!
"And, behold, thou shalt conceive in thy womb, and bring forth a son, and shalt call His name Jesus."
The name meant "the Lord saves." Jesus.
The angel was still speaking.
"He shall be great and shall be called the Son of the Highest: and the Lord God shall give unto Him the throne of His father, David: And He shall reign over the house of Jacob for ever; and of His kingdom there shall be no end."
With the implications of his words, Mary swallowed, her mind whirling.
Could this be? He was telling her she would bear the Messiah!
Unspeakable happiness gave her heart wings and, beating to God, it went soaring.
She felt immediately attacked by a chorus of dark voices as soon as the words were uttered. Her heart stopped. "Happiness and faith are not yours to have," she heard the voices secretly as they muttered:
"Why would the Lord choose you? Such a lowly peasant Nazarene girl. Ignore this madman. Look away from him. Reject what he's saying. Close your eyes! Say nothing!" In her mind these words began to quickly swirl.
Yet, came another voice that spoke; a very quiet voice her heart recognized and, with it, hope it did carry.
"What is your answer, my child Mary?"
Looking at the angel, she stood while tilting her head.
"How can I have a baby? I am a virgin; I've never shared my bed."
Smiling tenderly, the angel declared:

"The Holy Ghost shall come upon thee, and the power of the highest shall overshadow thee : therefore also that holy thing which shall be born of thee shall be called the Son of God.
And, behold, thy cousin Elizabeth, she hath also conceived a son in her old age: and this is the sixth month with her, who was called barren. For with God, nothing shall be impossible."
Mary drew in her breath with a radiating smile and clasped her hands. The angel of the Lord was asking her to be part of God's glorious plans.
And Mary said, "Behold the handmaid of the Lord; be it unto me according to thy word." And the angel departed from her.
As soon as she made her decision, the angel was gone. She uttered a soft gasp of dismay.
Shaken, she clutched her hands against her chest until she remembered the angel of the Lord had said not to be afraid.
Letting out her breath softly, she knelt and lifted her face to Heaven. With her palms up and hands lifted, she felt her heart swelling.
LORD, YOUR WILL BE DONE.
Her skin tingled strangely and was warmed with a flooding of sensation.
She drew in her breath and held it; for one brief space of time, nothing moved; no sound was heard as paused was all creation.
Within the womb of a poor peasant girl from an obscure village in Galilee, God the Son became one with the seed of Adam…
Mary: the girl whom God chose to be His Chosen through Obedience.

Chasms And Bridges Within The Heart

Found In The Eyes Of Serenity

Looking into the depths of pools overflowing with life's endless passions,
I find a youthful approach and a young heart beating with joyous compassions.
Young, free, and innocent the world seems to be.
Pain, hatred, and heartache have not yet been born; life's trials here are found not to see.
Endless love, longing affection, and deep admiration here abides,
Drawing you in ever closer like the waves of the oceans tides.
A peace falls over you here most divine and serene.
Here you find comfort and hope for the future; here you're always free to dream.
Full of brightness and an everlasting light that through all darkness always shines,
The life of this young one is like a never ending poem when with each and every passing day is always seeking its continuous rhymes.
Looking here, I can't help but wonder what her future will be,
A writer, a singer, a dancer?
Oh, all the possibilities that I am able to see!
Here, I find myself accepted despite all of my faults and flaws.
I have found my meaning in life; God has through the darkness answered all of my prayers and calls.

Amanda Perry

A longing for my presence,
A meaning for my very essence,
A thirst for my guidance and help,
A love everlasting here for me is most definitely felt.
Here, I am not just an ordinary person; but a mother, role model, and best friend.
Nothing can ever come between us; nothing will ever make this relationship end.
A yearning for knowledge is beginning to quickly grow,
Springing forth like a fountain of sustaining water with a never ceasing flow.
Here in her world, I truly wish you could see, my friend,
The happiness, the peace, and the love that I am blessed to see.
God, I have found, here comes before all else first,
Not because she's been forced in religion, but simply because in Him she does believe.
Reflecting back at me is strength in beautiful and caring eyes.
Here, I can proudly say, my heart has been stolen and never again free to give away.
I feel the endless love radiating through small and gentle hands
That fit into mine just right, never thinking about leaving but is forever with me to stay.
When the day is done and over, and she's sleeping by my side,
I find myself smiling gently and my heart swells with pride.
How thankful and blessed I am for God chose me to help in her creation.
These things found in the eyes of Serenity blesses me each day and night and fills my entire being with elation.

Chasms And Bridges Within The Heart

This poem is written for my only daughter: Serenity Leigh Battle.

She's my everything, my reason for living, and my comforter and best friend. I wanted to capture the emotion of gazing into her big brown eyes, but there really are no words to express the beauty that her eyes now hold. She truly is a blessing from God, and she loves me unconditionally. I used to try to imagine my future without children because a doctor once told me I would never be able to conceive, carry, and give birth due to my disorder with bulimia. How sad and lonely my future had seemed to become. Then a miracle happened that was from God: I became pregnant with a little baby girl. I love her more than anything and would not be able to survive life without her.

I love you, big baby girl, for now and forever!!!!!
Mommy

Amanda Perry

Life Changing Reflections

Vast oceans of endless love are found through open doors painted a bright, crystal hue of sparkling blue.
Through those two doors is never found any weakness; only comfort, hope, and tremendous strength that to your soul renews.
Found through the inside of these doors is laughter and young wisdom to be taught.
God's presence abides here always; here, one of His most precious angels can forever be sought.
God's amazing grace heavily sustaining,
Drawing people in; endless relationships are always quickly obtaining.
Qualities of serene tranquility,
Passion, love, perseverance; nothing is lost, blessed is every and all ability.
Dazzling insights of our Savior's Heaven are found here.
Blessed and full of honour are we to gaze through these doors for yet another year.
To enter into these doors with love and acceptance are no objections,
Found here inside a beautiful little boy's eyes are Life Changing Reflections…

Chasms And Bridges Within The Heart

This poem is extremely special because it was written for my nephew, Noah James Martin. His birthday is Sunday, and he will be five years old. Noah has taught our family so much. He taught us to love life, no matter what happens. He taught us to be strong, to remain faithful to God, and to love one another with an endless passion.

Noah was born with a very rare chromosome disorder. He's been in and out of doctor's offices his whole young life. When he was born, they discovered the disorder along with a broken leg. It was a trying time for his parents and family, but God gave little Noah a very special reason to be here...

We were told that Noah would never walk, but he defeated the odds against him. Today, not only can he walk, but he can run and run very fast, lol. He has survived many different medications, seizures, and even heart surgery. Noah is just turning five. He is a miracle; a blessing. I wrote this poem for Noah because every time I look into his beautiful eyes, I am reminded of the paintings of Christ's eyes.

It's as if Noah is actually way older and has wisdom unknown when you look into his eyes. He is amazingly compassionate and loves to hear and talk about Jesus and angels. The song sung by the group Alabama now comes to my mind: Angels Among Us.

God has blessed us with an angel in human form...

Happy birthday, Noah! We love you more than anything! Remain strong and never lose your childlike faith... you're here for a special reason, and that reason will be revealed in God's due season...

Amanda Perry

Glory

You can hear it in the whispering of the winds.
You can hear it in the motion of the trees limbs.
You can hear it in the symphony of a bird's song.
You can hear it all around you, and you finally realize that you belong.

Jesus, show me Your Glory.
Jesus, show me Your Glory.
Let the heavens open up and pour down showers of Your Mercy and Grace.
Jesus, show me Your Glory.
Jesus, show me Your Glory.
Let the showers wipe away all of the pain and all of the suffering until there's not left a single trace.

You can see it in your daughters big, bright eyes.
You can see it in the vastness of the skies.
You can see it in your own reflection.
You can see it all around you, and you finally realize that you have His affection.

Chasms And Bridges Within The Heart

Jesus, show me Your Glory.
Jesus, show me Your Glory.
Let the heavens open up and pour down showers of Your Mercy and Grace.
Jesus, show me Your Glory.
Jesus, show me Your Glory.
Let the showers wipe away all of the pain and all of the suffering until there's not left a single trace.

You can feel it in the depths of your soul.
You can feel it in the precious Book that you now hold.
You can feel it surrounding all of your prayers, and you finally realize that for you someone important cares.

Jesus, show me Your Glory.
Jesus, show me Your Glory.
Let the heavens open up and pour down showers of Your Mercy and Grace.
Jesus, show me Your Glory.
Jesus, show me Your Glory.
Let the showers wipe away all of the pain and all of the suffering until there's not left a single trace.

Showers of Your Mercy and Grace.
Falling on each and every face.
Thank You, Lord, for leading me to this place.
Jesus, show me Your Glory
Jesus, show me Your Glory

Amanda Perry

Lord, I've surrendered my heart, and I've surrendered my soul.
I now live for that day when You call my name from Heaven's eternal scroll.
I now live my life for You.
I've been washed in Your Blood and I've been made new.

Jesus, use me for Your Glory.
Jesus, use me for Your Glory.
Let the heavens open up and pour down showers of Your Mercy and Grace.
Jesus, use me for Your Glory.
Jesus, use me for Your Glory.
Let the showers wipe away all of the pain and all of the suffering until there's not left a single trace.

Use me for Your Glory…
Jesus, use me…

Chasms And Bridges Within The Heart

Dying In Love

Life was finally falling into place.
She had actually found that special person who could make her heart race.
Sweet whispers of promises of forever and for always
Made her believe this one was different; he wasn't just for herself a phase.
He filled her full of comfort, passion, and happiness galore.
There was never anything in her life that she had wanted more.
On a beautiful star-filled night, he bent down upon one knee.
Her answer was:"Yes, your wife I will now and for always be!"
The wedding was short and very discrete;
She truly believed her knight in shining armor had come and had swept her off her feet.
It wasn't even a full day after being married that things began to change.
The man she knew and loved began acting very strange.
One minute, the man she had married was right there.
The next minute, a new and horrifying man was glaring at her through his hateful stare.

Amanda Perry

The first time it happened, it was an accident, he had said.
She stood before him trembling with fear and surprise as a current of blood flowed from the nose delicately placed upon her tormented head.
Promises of tomorrow, of better times than these, come from a pair of the most sinister of lips.
Her calls to her family were being monitored, they had to work the exact same schedule at the exact same place, and when he or his mother left, she found herself locked inside; depression quickly descends upon her, and into its arms she silently slips.

She tries to understand.
He tells her she's not thin enough, smart enough, nor pretty enough anymore and, being at his mercy, she suffers great abuse from his hand.
She became very ill.
Her gallbladder developed stones, and the pain was so severe herself she thought it would kill.
After the surgery when she went home,
Things just weren't right; they were horribly wrong.
He took her pain medication and birth control away from her and hid them.
The day after surgery, he climbed on top of her; she weakly tried to fight him off but it was a battle that she just could not win.
She surrendered fighting and went limp as behind her he tied her arms and then tied her legs
"Please, not today," she quietly hears herself beg.
He leaned his face down to hers and placed his teeth upon her lips,
Biting hard enough to draw sticky flowing blood.
Tears fell quickly as he continued downward biting and pinching, making pain surround her and drown her like a great flood.

Chasms And Bridges Within The Heart

He seemed to be the happiest when he was inflicting pain.
Like a super hero in a comic book, immense power he seemed to gain.
She trembled as he stopped and lit a cigarette instead.
He smiled as he took a few puffs, filling her being with great dread.
"I want a baby… a baby boy…" He suddenly said.
She watched in horror as he brought his cigarette just inches above her skin; slowly he brought it down and her skin burned and turned extremely red.
Her screams he violently choked off with the two of his hands.
She tried to stay quiet and follow each and every demand.
Suddenly, pain erupted, burning through to her very soul.
It felt as if her stitches from surgery had ripped open, and she felt lightheaded and dizzy as her body lost all control.
The organs within her body felt like they were going to explode.
Red and sticky liquid suddenly gushed free from below.
Still, he did not stop; still, he did not slow.
Fading in and out of consciousness, currents of searing and burning pain continued their merciless flow.
Finally, waking up sometime after,
She gazed at her body and saw sublime disaster.
Big blue, purple, and black bruises were everywhere.
She choked back a sob as she looked down and stared.
She was lying in her own pool of blood.
She felt extremely dirty and could imagine and visualize herself covered in mud.
Tenderly and slowly, she showered and the bed clothes she did manage to clean.

Amanda Perry

He was not there now but probably at the bar; the quietness around her was soothing and serene.
She slowly made the bed.
Then gingerly laid herself back down because now throbbing with pain was her head.
She lay like that for two whole days.
She had thought a lot; planned her own escape in many different ways.
Her grandmother and mother came to visit on the third day.
She found herself going back to her roots but at the old farmhouse was she afraid to stay.
So, they went to visit family in Kentucky.
She started realizing that she had survived quite a lot; from then on, she considered herself very lucky.
Weeks quickly passed, and each day she grew stronger.
She could not put it off anymore; she had to go back to West Virginia; a divorce just could not wait any longer.
To be free of him forever and to suffer no more abuse at his hands
Made her mind realize he was killing her slowly; I have to do this to save my life, her mind and soul demands.
She was granted the divorce and quickly it went through.
Domestic violence is on the rise, so I felt led to share my own story with you.
If you are going through this please know that you are not ALONE.
There is a way out, and there's love for you to be shown.
Keep your head held up high and remain strong.
You'll be feeling victorious now, it won't be very long.

Secret Friend

I met a new friend, today.
She is amazing at making me forget, and she even erases all of my troubles away.
With her I find myself being happy, calm, and well-collected.
Without her I feel myself being depressed, agitated, and eerily rejected.
It seems as if my new friend, well, she honestly understands me.
She takes me from Rock Bottom, and up onto the top of the world we quickly flee.
She fills me with such confidence, such energy, and such delight.
Best friends quickly we're becoming and to go a day without her, well, honestly it just doesn't seem right.
Choices are easier to make when I have her by my side.
When I'm with her, my true self I no longer now have to hide.
She accepts me as I am, even with all of my flaws.
From the moment that I wake up until I drift back to sleep again, she's always there; my name she always calls.
Days quickly pass and turn into weeks.
Every hour of every day and every night, my secret friend is who my mind seeks.
It's as if I'm obsessed with her, and I have to always keep her in my sight.

Amanda Perry

No one else can see her; she's all mine, you see. I've taken to being always alone and by myself in darkness, instead of being in the light.
We have some great times, my secret friend and I.
Most, I can't even remember, and now I'm confused because my bank account has gone completely dry.
What am I without my secret friend?
How am I to make it through the entire day and entire night without her holding my hand?
Panic grips my trembling shoulders with an iron clasp.
Suddenly, tears well up within my eyes and uncontrollably I start to shudder, and for life's precious breath I begin to gasp.

The next week is very trying for me.
Not once my secret friend have I been able to see.
I've been depressed and extremely sad.
My temper is short and absolutely everything makes me mad.
I have no appetite; it's quite impossible to eat.
I feel as if I've been knocked off of the course in my own life; I find it hard to march to my own heart's drum beat.
I have to find a way, so I gather all my DVD movie discs and hurry down to the nearest pawn shop to sell them; I have to make some quick cash.
My secret friend and I are going to party; we're going to have a great big bash…

Chasms And Bridges Within The Heart

Something is different about my secret friend, this time.
In her company, tonight, I feel depressed and worthless.
For some reason, I'm getting mad and extremely furious.
She keeps bringing up bad memories of my past.
I should have known that our great friendship was just too good to be true; it just wasn't made to forever last.
Disgusted with myself, I push my friend away.
Then, memories of our good times together play through my head, so I grab her and pull her back to me closely to stay...
My friends and family ask me what's going on in my life.
I try to hide behind my secret friend and tell them that I'm just not sleeping enough at night.
The thing about friends and family is that they know your true self way too well.
"We know about your friend," they say, and immediately my face fell.
How could they possibly know about her? I wondered as I finally broke down.
"I need some help," these words were extremely hard to be found.
ALCOHOL...
That's my secret friend's name.
Instead of happiness, she started bringing me physical and mental pain.
Thankfully for me, my friends and family did intervene.
As for my secret friend, well, I found that without her my life continues to bloom and to succeed.

Amanda Perry

Comfort On A Cloud

As I bow my head and clasp my hands, to God the Father I begin to pray.
I'm filled with an overflowing joy that radiates from head to toe and on my face paints a flashing smile that's permanently fixed to always now and forever stay.
Closing my eyes, I now feel a calmness and peace enveloping me.
Lord, I'm filled with a thirst for You; my only desire is to You to be close, as close as can possibly be…
Everything around me suddenly fades into a mist, swirling and disappearing.
I hold my breath and listen; listen for what You, my God, will now be to me revealing.
Oh, to stand in such peaceful tranquility,
I find myself exhaling breaths, humility.
My body is Your Holy Temple.
To give my all to You, Lord, now feels so easy and so simple.
I stand in awesome wonder as I feel Your loving arms embrace me.
I feel as if I'm being carried away from this earth to a far away beautiful place that only Your chosen can see.
Listen… I hear the whispers in the wind,
"Do not be afraid, for I am holding your hand; do not fear, Amanda, my friend."

Chasms And Bridges Within The Heart

Comfort… endless comfort and amazing love engulf my entire being.
I slowly open my eyes and cannot believe what it is I'm seeing…
A vast expanse of an open and endless sky.
Colors of the rainbow shimmering all throughout the clouds paints a portrait most dazzling; so beautiful, I begin to cry.
I smell a sweet fragrance that's not of this world and, when inhaling, immediately it brings all your senses alive.
There's an electric current that fills the air, and suddenly I'm moving; I gaze down around me and smile as I find myself seated upon a cloud, enjoying this miraculous ride.
The world below me seems so tiny and so small.
Words will never be able to describe such beauty; no, no words at all.
A figure tall stands right before me.
Robes of pure white glisten from the brilliant light that surrounds His entire being; the light is so dazzling that His face I cannot see.
Fear?
What is fear?
It can and will never be found here.
"Lord, who am I that You have blessed and allowed to see such things?"
His voice is pure and gentle and along with it comes a melodious ring.
"Amanda, you are my daughter in whom I am well pleased."
"You have suffered much and have come a long way; you opened your entire being unto Me, and you believe."
I fell to my knees, overcome with emotion.
"Lord, I want to do Your will; to You I surrender my all, and I give You everything I have. But most of all I, give You all of my devotion."
I feel a sense of belonging and compassion as His hand He reaches out to me.

Amanda Perry

I am filled with sheer amazement and wonder at the scar on His hand I now can finally see.
Gruesome and gory?
What is gruesome and gory?
Here, it is nothing; looking at His scar, I stand in awe of God's wondrous glory.
A feeling of astonishment suddenly overtakes my being.
I gasp at the scar on His hand, and I'm filled with sadness and amazement at this most precious sight I'm now seeing.
The scar on His hand is not healed and stabbed even after all these years.
Instead, the scar appears to be brand new, flowing freely with His precious, saving blood; pain as if from a sword quickly through my heart sears.
"Lord, I am not worthy to stand in Your presence and feel Your glory radiating all around me."
"Please, have a seat and take comfort on a cloud, for there's something that you must see."
Comfort and peace fall down in sparkling showers all around me.
I'm not afraid as I gaze into His scar and find that it's His own ascension into Heaven that I so clearly can see.
"In that day was I taken up and received by a cloud."
Visions then started playing like a movie before my very eyes,
Showing the world in its bitter past and flowing into its gruesome present; the visions stop suddenly, and all around me I can hear the people's prayers and cries.
So much hatred, so much murder, so much pain.
Christians everywhere are crying out to God to save them, their family, their friends; Jesus we need You like the drought needs the rain.

Chasms And Bridges Within The Heart

"Lord, how much longer shall we suffer through all of this evil?"
"You must tarry yet a little while, but look to the clouds for you know not at what time I'm coming; because for you to know is inconceivable."
"Amanda, the people need to hear,"
"Your purpose now is becoming very clear."
I close my eyes and nod my head.
"You have been blessed with a talent that you must use to reach out to other people before I come back," are the words that He said.
"Lord, You are my God, my Father, in You do I truly believe; I am alive and here today for a reason: to do Your will and to share Your light burning within me."
"Lord, Thy will be done; I will not fear, for I put my trust completely in Thee."
I gazed around and found that I was still on my knees down beside my bed; where I had started to pray…
Smiling inside and out, I opened my curtains back and prayed a prayer of thanks as I made leave to start my day…

Amanda Perry

Feeding The Flame Of The Fire

What is your main reason for being alive?
For some it is wealth, fortune, and fame; but there's a much better choice that we are free to choose: To live life for God… that's what choice I've come to decide.
When Jesus comes into your heart,
Your whole world changes; it's no longer falling apart.
He comes into your heart and cleanses and makes it completely new.
Deep within your soul, a fire has been kindled, and along with it comes a new desire, too.
To live life only for God the Father and do His perfect will.
When you surrender your all to Him, locked doors start to open and what's inside only God can and will reveal.
The fire starts burning, and great miracles soon begin to develop.
Passion and desire flame up within your soul; the passion and desire for a living and loving God all around you soon does envelop.
There is found within your soul great burning sensations.
To read and hear God's Holy word fills your soul with multiple elations.
A yearning develops; a burning sensation to become closer with the Lord.

Chasms And Bridges Within The Heart

The flame that feeds the fire becomes stronger, causing a great rebirth of flames that burn throughout your soul and cuts through your heart like a gleaming double-edged sword.
The fire within you releases within your body Christ's most radiant light.
Your eyes become brighter, and your happiness seems to explode; just like placing a match to a stick of dynamite.

What is your main reason for being alive?
To make sure the fire is always kindled and burning bright is what God's chosen have come to decide.
Let the fire always burn.
Let the soul always and forever yearn.
The world we live in is full of sinister darkness and the devil's hate.
The fire within your soul provides light for those around you, making them stop to think twice about their own fate.
The fire in your soul is like a brightly burning beacon in the dead of night;
Always burning, always bringing those lost in the darkness to the light.
To be an example, to share my light from God's purifying fire is what I pray for every day.
God has answered my prayers by using my body as His Willing Vessel;
His gift of writing He has bestowed upon me, and I pray that reading it will change your life in a brand new way.
The flame that feeds the fire within your soul has awesome and magnificent power.

Amanda Perry

It will save you from eternal destruction; it will be the burning light in your darkest hour.
To the murderer, it brings redemption and saving grace.
To the depressed, it brings happiness and a permanent smile upon the face.
To the drug addict, it brings a new high; a new raging desire.
To the prostitute, it brings love and cleansing and burns up the old life which is covered in the muck and mire.

What was John the Baptist's main reason for being alive?
He was a great prophet and doing God's will every day, he did strive.
He had a passion, a yearning, and a fire sent from above abiding in him.
His goal was to teach the people that there is a way to escape and live away from sin.
He was to pave the way for a much stronger Light that would come to this earth to bless.
This Light was fueled by God's endless love and devotedness.

What was Jesus the Christ's main reason for being alive?
To bring the universe everlasting light and to guide the people to live in goodness, instead of sin, He did strive.
He had a Neverending Fire burning deep within His beautiful soul.
He took the blackness from the sinners' hearts and made it new and pure white, so no longer would the heart be black as the blackest coal.
The Flame of Fire within Jesus was fueled by His everlasting Father, and His purpose to do His Father's will.

Chasms And Bridges Within The Heart

Satan tempted and tried Jesus many different times, but the fire that Jesus has, Satan was and will never be able to kill.
The more Jesus walked among the people here on earth and the more He preached and taught,
Great multitudes came and listened to His every Word and with them Jesus shared His Neverending fire that throughout all of history could never be bought.
From generation down through generation, Jesus Christ has fueled these raging fires.
He has awakened people's slumbering hearts and has filled them with righteous desires.
As Jesus was beaten and mocked and scorned,
His Fire never died… if anything, the love He had for every person on this earth enabled a new brilliant blazing fire to be reborn.
When Jesus was nailed to the cross, His Fire didn't even seem to dwindle.
Knowing He was taking away the sins of the world; bold new flames began in Him to rekindle.

What is the Christian's main reason for being alive?
As we all know, the world we live in today seems to be most embracing of the darkness. As Christians, we have the flaming fire within us; it's impossible to hide.
Everything we say and do should bring Glory to the Lord – should become the fuel that's feeding the flame of the fire that deep within us lie.

Amanda Perry

As Christians, we all have one thing in common: Fire; it's a bond that will never break but will forever remain tied.
It's time for us all to stand up and be strong.
We need to re-teach the world on what's right and what's wrong.
Rekindle the fire within us to bring it to its brilliant blaze,
So that our lights shine brilliantly and steadfastly so we can witness sinners changing their ways.
As Christians, through the darkness we each must fight.
The battle between God and Satan rages throughout every day and throughout every night.
This battle will last until the end of time;
Until Jesus Christ comes back and splits the people of the world into two separate lines.
The first line is to be filled with God's people; true Christians who fed the flame of the fire and always kept it burning.
The second line is to be filled with the tormented and the damned; people who had the chance to find their light but loved the world instead and never a new leaf in their life turning.
So, as people here on earth, we have a very important choice to make.
Are you going to follow God and ignite that fire within, or are you going to dwell in darkness and be chained in the bottom less pit of eternal fire… burning… burning… burning… the choice is yours, which path will you take?

The Dragon's Lair

An endless abyss of lurking shadows and unthinkable nightmares,
The walls and floors have ears and eyes it seems; this place is alive and to it nothing can and never will be able to compare.
Suffocating darkness closes in;
Garments being torn and ripped from shadows hiding from deep within.
The floor seems to begin twisting and coiling just like a snake.
Slithering, scurrying, and creeping are the sounds the walls and floors make.
Standing stark still and silent here in time,
Darkness, darkness, darkness: any brilliant form of light here never can or will shine.
Warm, sticky, and oozing liquid drip in sprinkles from the ceiling, the color of a rich and dark red.
Drip… drip… drip… dripping onto your confused and frightened head.
From the ground in the center of the room suddenly forms a massively burning fire.
Terror seizes your soul as escaping alive becomes your one and only desire.

Amanda Perry

In the far right corner, a small child's form can be seen.
She appears to be frightened and trembling; across her forehead, sweat leaves a most glistening sheen.
You cautiously walk over to her and place your hand upon her small arm.
She looks up at you and smiles, then giggles, and then hysterically laughs. "Welcome to Hell," she says as her laughter seems to sound an alarm.
Before your very eyes the girl starts to transform.
Where minutes before sat a little girl appears now a black shadow, very grotesque and very forlorn.
Its eyes appear to be two big drops of the richest blood red.
Not just two develop, but seven more glare at you from on top of its head.
It opens its mouth, and you see rows upon rows of sharp and jagged, bloodstained teeth.
It slowly saunters over to you and raises its arms like a child wanting to be carried; you shake your head and then it laughs… "Behold, the king's angels are released."
The room begins to shake and to severely tremble.
Losing your balance onto the bloodstained and dirty floor, you quickly fall; the Shadow seizes the moment and sinks its multiple teeth into your leg; teeth sharper than the sharpest spindle.
A ravishing poison quickly runs through your veins.
Searing, burning, and unbearable so strong are the pains.
The fire in the center of the floor suddenly blazes and flares.
Out of the fire come three enormous creatures and, when they see you, they hungrily stare.

Chasms And Bridges Within The Heart

They are nothing that has ever been seen before.
Covering their immense body are glistening scales of multicolored hues. Smearing across their snouts are all forms of human blood and gore.
A chorus of howling erupts through the stifling air.
Along with the howling creatures suddenly erupts millions of screams; screams of tortured despair.
They move in unison as if one terrible being,
Circling around you and crouching down as if you are the prey that they will soon be feasting.
Sheer terror unables you to run away.
As they stop and stare, your nostrils fill up with the scent of molding and rotting decay.
They all attack together and at the same time,
Ripping and shredding with no reason nor rhyme.
You feel bones being broken and pulled away from their socket.
You hear the blood pulsating through your ears like the roaring of a space rocket.
You wait for the oblivion of unconsciousness; that place between life and death where surrounding darkness and relaxing silence is located.
Woozy and dizzy, you gaze around and realize that the entire room with your own blood has now been saturated.
Ripping...
Tearing...
Screaming to release the pain...
Burning...
Searing...
You wait for the darkness of death to grip your soul but it is never for you to gain...

Amanda Perry

The fire crackled and flared: "Return my pets," declares an eerily smooth and relaxed voice.
The deadly creatures obey and vanish into the fire as if they have no other choice.
Almost every bone in your body has been splintered and shattered. You shriek and scream from the tormenting pain; every inch of your body feels to be sliced through completely and scattered.
"Why?"
"Why?!"
"Lord…"
"Kill me!"
"Please, just kill me!"
A dark and demonic laugh slithers slowly into the room.
All around you, the bleeding walls begin slowly melting; horrifying realizations come to mind: You are Doomed…
A blast of scorching heat suddenly engulfs your whole mangled body. Immediately, your mouth becomes parched and you lick your lips, which from your blood tastes extremely salty.
The walls have melted away and now you gaze upon an endless lake of burning fire.
In the midst of this lake, you see a very beautiful man seated upon a throne made out of glistening gold and red rubies; he's sitting in the burning flames and, yet, he doesn't expire.
His beauty is magical and breathtaking.
You exhale a breath as the pain from your body leaves.
"Come, my pet," says this man as he opens his arms up for me to willingly receive.

Chasms And Bridges Within The Heart

I lie on the floor and shake my head.
This man is beautiful but somehow he fills you with sudden dread.
He smiles and glides quickly toward you.
"Please, be still and I will make your broken body new."
You stare at the man's face while your body quickly begins to heal.
"What is this place?"
"Who are you?"
He laughs and helps you up to your feet.
"My darling dear, follow me and I will indeed give to thee a treat."
Your body refuses to follow the man.
As if reading your mind, he laughs merrily and at you he angrily stares as back into the center of the fire he now proudly stands.
He begins to chant in a language unheard of and as if seeking worship, he raises his hands.
Appearing suddenly throughout the fire, creatures and monsters now all around him stands.
Demonic chanting rings through both of your ears.
The man fixes his eyes upon you and quickly awakens all of your fears.
Eyes begin to change color and shape.
A hideous snout takes the place of his nose and great billows of raging smoke his nostrils now make.
A serpent's great slithering tongue glides over teeth glistening white as snow and that are as sharp as a needle's point.
The temperature suddenly rises, and your bones feel as if they are melting. Searing pain blazes through each and every joint.

Amanda Perry

Terrible screaming and intensified wailing rise up with the blazing flames.
Appearing now in the lake of fire, surrounding a menacing dragon, you see millions of people crying for help; you tremble and honestly believe that you are insane.
The dragon is enormous and breathes great blazes of fire.
In its blood-red eyes, you see the greatest passions for destroying and killing its greatest and only desire.
A great rumbling erupted from the dragon's immense throat.
A mighty and applied voice shook the whole entire place: "My friends, get ready…
The time is coming… that evil shall defeat all," he clearly and excitedly spoke.
Creatures, monsters, and demons began a wild and provocative dance.
"Come and join me…"
"I am too powerful… Evil will indeed conquer all…"
"This is your final chance…"
You shake your head, absolutely terrified.
The dragon roars and blows fire in your direction; you flinch and close your eyes, believing that here in Hell you truly died.
You open your eyes to see familiar surroundings; shaking with fear, it was just a dream you slowly begin to realize…

Essence Of Writing

It has become a part of you.
You involve it in everything that you say and do.
It flows through your veins, making a permanent resident deep within your heart.
It has become your life and with it you can never part.
It has become the air you breathe.
You find in it the strength and comfort that you daily need.
A form of therapy it is to a weary soul.
A crutch to lean on, it helps you in regaining control.
It has become your life's awesome purpose.
A window to your soul, it allows a view of your entire being, not just what's on the surface.
It has become your special talent; your hidden gift.
It's what you use to help suffering and to encouragingly uplift.
It has become a part of your family; a very wonderfully-advising best friend.
One who will always guide you along life's every curve and winding bend.
It has become your inspiring creations.
To your soul it brings glorious and uplifting elations.
It has become your hope and dreams.
Great and fulfilling satisfaction to your very life it does always bring.
It has become a sweet possession that you delight in.
It defines you; your essence of writing.

Amanda Perry

Heavenly Gift

Sparkling ribbons of ecstatic delight;
The key to the heart in tiny hands is held tight.
Precious moments of blissful love;
Heavenly glow radiates and surrounds a most wondrous gift sent down from up above.
Born from innocent tinkling laughter, tiny fairies soon take flight.
Tiny but loyal guardians are they of the star-filled night.
Gentle butterfly kisses tickle and warm the skin.
Sheer bliss and joyful radiance rise into sight and a most dazzling dance does begin.
Undying love and acceptance radiate promising light from deep within.
Broken and shattered heart is healing and learning how to love once again...
Into your life, immense happiness and joy she does bring,
Making your heart swell up with love and beautifully sing.
Glittering crystal-blue eyes hold the power to draw you in.
Warming comfort and permanent peace to you she freely does lend.
Innocent beauty engulfs her being, all around.
A glimpse of Heaven here on earth is the aura that around her surrounds.
Warm and satin smooth is her skin to the touch.
How can something so little and small be loved so much?
Radiating and sublime bliss now in your life holds a special place.
Little angel from Heaven, my niece.
Chanel Anniston, life's saving grace.

Reflective Deception

She stands before the mirror.
She frowns to herself as her own reflection now becomes, to her weakened and sad eyes, distinctly clearer.
Gazing back at herself are two eyes blazing with accusation and extreme hatred.
What happened to her innocence?
What happened to all the things that to her once appeared so sacred?
She used to enjoy life.
Never a part of it were hardships and strife.
Life used to be different; life used to be innocent and great.
What happened to cause within herself so much pain and so much hate?
In reality, her reflection is slowly dying.
To be accepted, to be loved, and to be beautiful she diligently and faithfully has been trying.
Eyes have become sunken and weakly deep-set upon her head,
Ghostly pale and always shivering from staying cold.
She now spends her days covered up in her bed.
Wasting away to nothing over one hundred pounds she has now quickly lost.
She tells herself that gaining happiness must always come with a cost.

Amanda Perry

Her clothes no longer fit upon her continually-shrinking frame.
Her eyes are lifeless and very dim, no longer lit up by a burning flame.
Protruding from her skin in many different angles are her skeleton's bones.
Yet every time she gazes in the mirror, she angrily and sadly moans…
The person she sees in the mirror is full of hateful anger.
Her own worst enemy she has become but remains inconspicuous of the destructive danger.
Reflecting back at her is a girl with way too much fat here and there.
Clothes that are way too tight show every curve and every inch of extra skin; always making people gaze and at her intently stare.
She finds hidden within herself a daily raging battle,
Losing her sanity as in her head the angry voices begin their endless prattle:
Worthless and plain,
Life for her has nothing at all to ever gain.
Undeserving of any and all forms of love, especially love and affection sent from the Father up above…
Reflective deception is sadly what nourishes this growing obsession.

Temptation

Surrounded by nature and all of her melodious sounds,
His full attention was given unto His Father as He sat quietly down on
His knees upon the lushly-carpeted ground.
He remained drawn to His Father in deep concentration, like this, for
forty days and forty nights.
He never once ventured away nor allowed His prayers to cease; to His
faith He always held on tight.
A rushing wind swept through the wilderness where He sat.
His heart began to beat more furiously as held deep within; His chest, it
felt cornered and trapped.
Suddenly, He became aware of the emptiness within His stomach, and
the thought of eating was conquering all other thoughts.
Something evil was lurking in the shadows and His beautiful body
shudders at the power this something has along with it brought.
He takes a deep breath to calm His shaking hands.
The smell of burning fire and rotting flesh engulf Him as before Him a
dark and menacing shadow now silently and eerily stands.
He suddenly became overwhelmed by His empty stomach and the
desire to find food.
He rolled onto the ground and silently began to pray; the shadow came
closer and hysterically laughed, becoming very rude.

Amanda Perry

A voice broke through the silence, very smooth and dripping with dread,
"If thou be the Son of God, command that these stones be made bread."
He faced the shadow and saw right through his facade,
"It is written, Man shall not live by bread alone, but by every word that proceedeth out of the mouth of God."
The shadow hissed and transformed into a pale white man,
A great wind and mist enveloped the two men as the pale one stretched out his claw-like hands.
They were now in the Holy city, standing on top of a pinnacle of the temple.
The pale man smiled because to tempt this great man before him was, in fact, so simple.
As he spoke, his eyes turned the color of blood, and his lips became covered with bloody foam.
"If thou be the Son of God, cast thy self down: for it is written, He shall give His angels charge concerning thee: and in their hands they shall bear thee up, lest at any time thou dash thy foot against a stone."
The other man closed His beautiful blue eyes and silently gave a gentle nod.
"It is written again, Thou shalt not tempt the Lord thy God."
A desperate and aggravated shriek escaped from foam-covered lips.
The pale man's skin started to rip, and away from his body it quickly started to drip.
Thickening mists and violent winds took them both even higher and up onto the top of a mountain.
Violent shudders and tormented screams flowed up through the pale man's throat and erupted like water in a fountain.

Chasms And Bridges Within The Heart

He no longer had the pale white skin.
In its place, gruesome and slimy scales forming now did begin.
He wasn't a man, at all... a creature, maybe...
Satan! Of course, the Devil he was certain to be.
He glared at the other man who stood next to him, full of calmness and peace.
He showed this man all the kingdoms of this world, and by using the glory of them, he soon began to tempt and to tease.
"All these things will I give thee, if thou wilt fall down and worship me."
Voice growing stronger the man replied:
"Get thee hence, Satan: for it is written, Thou shalt worship the Lord thy God, and Him only shalt thou serve."
As soon as these last words were spoken, the Devil vanished and beautiful angels descended from Heaven to administer to Jesus the care that He did deserve.

Amanda Perry

The Blessed Hope

Therefore be ye also ready: For in such an hour as ye think not the Son of man cometh. **(Matthew 24:44)**

A young couple stands before a preacher, reciting precious wedding vows.
Suddenly, the entire congregation disappears, including the preacher and bride; a scream ripples through the silence as to his knees the groom mercifully bows.

A mother soon-to-be smiles as she cradles her growing belly.
Suddenly, her stomach goes flat as the precious gift of life so freely given now has been taken away; the mother surrenders herself over to unconsciousness as her body becomes shaky like jelly.

A teenager maybe sixteen or seventeen now sits at the family's dining room table, alone.
Just minutes before, his younger sister had been blowing out her fourth birthday candles; turning over the table in a fit of rage, the boy falls to the floor and endlessly moans.

Chasms And Bridges Within The Heart

A preacher falls to his knees as before his very eyes his whole congregation disappears.
His heart fills with pain as if it has been pierced through with a sharpened spear.

A teacher turns away from the math problem written on the black board and faces her now empty room.
Her heart beats wildly as her soul quickly fills with impending doom.

On a plane, over the Atlantic, passengers scream and begin to hysterically cry.
The plane suddenly veers off course and dives down toward the earth; without the pilot and Co-pilot, they are all destined to tragically die.

Confusion...
Chaos...
Terror...
Disaster...

The world is falling apart, is being destroyed, is coming to an end.
Screams...
Screams of pain, screams of grief, and screams of endless mourning take flight on the whispers of the wind.
It seems as if the world has ceased it's turning.
While all Hell now on earth breaks loose, raging and kindling its ceaseless and constant burning.

Amanda Perry

The Son of Perdition laughs and celebrates as the world becomes evil;
as evil as can possibly be.
He quickly gains immense power and his monsters and his demons he
excitedly up on the now troubled earth begins to set free.

Hate…
Greed…
Lust…
Death…

The world has no order and is quickly going insane.
Rape, murder, theft; the world cries out for shelter from all of the
endless pain.
People are looking for answers; walking around confused and dazed.
Millions upon millions have suddenly vanished and have quickly
vanished without even a single trace.
Power outages are all over the entire universe.
All forms of communication have been wiped out, and all forms of
transportation have either been destroyed or are stuck in place, neither
moving forward or driving in reverse.
All over the world, millions have vanished; how are we to now cope?

The Blessed Hope…
The Blessed Hope…

Chasms And Bridges Within The Heart

A world now no longer blessed by the little children's purity and lovingness.
A world now no longer warmed by the sweet breath of a baby; never again to feel the softness of a baby's gentle caress.
A world filled with the dying and the deceased.
A world now yearning for unity and everlasting peace...

One of the most compelling prophetic events in the Bible is called the "Rapture" of the church. The apostle Paul provides us with most of the available details:

But I would not have you to be ignorant, brethern, concerning them which are asleep, that ye sorrow not, even as others which have no hope.
For if we believe that Jesus died and rose again, even so them also which sleep in Jesus will God bring with Him.
For this we say unto you by the word of the Lord, that we which are alive and remain unto the coming of the Lord shall not prevent them which are asleep.
For the Lord Himself shall descend from Heaven with a shout, with the voice of the archangel and with the trump of God: and the dead in Christ shall rise first:
Then we which are alive and remain shall be caught up together with them in the clouds, to meet the Lord in the air: and so shall we ever be with the Lord. Wherefore comfort one another with these words.
(1 Thessalonians 4:13-18)

In *(1 Corinthians 15:51-52)* Paul unveiled what he called a "Mystery"- that Christians "shall all be changed (transformed) in a moment, in the twinkling of an eye." This mystery was revealed primarily by the apostle Paul.

In the Old Testament, Enoch provides an illustration of this transforming experience:

> *And Enoch walked with God: and he was not; for God took him.*
> ***(Genesis 5:24)***

A day is coming when all believers will be transformed like the godly Enoch, whose earthly body was suddenly made fit to be in Heaven with God. In Paul's terms, this happens when "this corruptible (our bodies) has put on incorruption, and this mortal has put on immortality." *(1 Corinthians 15:54)* The Rapture, I believe, is not only for those Christians who "are alive and remain" at the coming of Christ, but includes all believers from the day of Pentecost to the day Christ returns for His church.

> *Looking for that blessed hope, and the glorious appearing of the great God and our Savior Jesus Christ:* ***(Titus 2:13)***

That is exactly what the Rapture is; a Blessed Hope. When the Bible uses the word "hope" here, it does not mean a nice thing we earnestly suspect might happen, but rather a certified fact of the future, promised by God's unfailing Word. In this case, "hope" means a present and confident expectation of a certain important future event.

"The Blessed Hope" could very well refer uniquely to the snatching up of believers just prior to the beginning of the Tribulation. Then again, it could also refer to the Resurrection when all believers will be raised to live with God for eternity, where they will be with their loved ones who share their faith in Christ. Or, I suppose it could be both, for they are both a "Blessed Hope" to Christians and are designed by God to "comfort" His children. *(1 Thessalonians 4:18)*

One of the chief characteristics of the Rapture of the church is that it will be sudden, unexpected, and will catch people by complete surprise. As our Lord said, "No man knows the day or the hour." Which is why we should live so as to "be ready, for the Son of Man is coming at an hour when you do not expect Him." *(Matthew 24:44)* Nothing is a better motivator than to believe Jesus could come at any moment!

For if we believe that Jesus died and rose again, even so them also which sleep in Jesus will God bring with him. (1 Thessalonians 4:14)

And if you are wondering what you must do to have this blessed hope, the answer is simple:

Believe in the death of Christ for all of our sins and His resurrection! If you do not currently believe this, I urge you to confess your sins directly to Jesus Christ and invite Him into your life and heart to become your Lord and Savior:

Dear Heavenly Father,

I believe you sent your Son Jesus to die on the cross for my sins and the sins of the world. I also believe You raised Him from the dead and that He is soon coming again to set up His Kingdom. Therefore, today I confess my sin of rebellion to You and invite Jesus into my heart to become my Lord and Savior. I give myself to You, Jesus, and that I would like to serve You as long as I live.

Amen.

Amanda Perry

Seeing then that all these things shall be dissolved, what manner of persons ought ye to be in all holy conversation and godliness,
Looking for and hasting unto the coming of the day of God, wherein the heavens being on fire shall be dissolved, and the elements shall melt with fervent heat?
Nevertheless we, according to his promise, look for new heavens and a new earth, where in dwelleth righteousness.
Wherefore, beloved, seeing that ye look for such things, be diligent that ye may be found of him in peace, without spot, and blameless.
(2 Peter 3:11-14)

But grow in grace, and in the knowledge of our Lord and Saviour Jesus Christ. To him be glory both now and for ever. Amen.
(2 Peter 3:18)

Wonderfully Made

I will praise thee; for I am fearfully and wonderfully made: marvelous are thy works: and that my soul knoweth right well. **(Psalm 139:14)**

For as long as I can remember,
My body to sickness and disease have I always surrendered.
Opening my soul freely to evil,
While hidden deep inside were all my tears, but showing freely on the outside I appeared to be most gleeful.
This disease your whole body it does take over.
Instead of bringing you up, it only brings you lower.
I realize that I was sacrificing my soul and body for hate.
For some, this realization comes way too late.
I wish with all of my heart I could have reached these young women and men.
Helped them to change their life; to see what they each could have been.
But I know there's no way that I can change the past.
Hopefully, with God's help, living in the present and future I can make an impression which will last...

Amanda Perry

Today's culture bombards us with messages about fashion, glamour, exercise, nutrition, and care of the body. The Bible, however, stresses inner beauty: "Your beauty should not come from outward adornment, such as braided hair and the wearing of gold jewelry and fine clothes. Instead, it should be that of your inner self, the unfading beauty of a gentle and quiet spirit." *(1 Peter 3:3-4)* This Christian principle is worth stressing again in a society that often measures women by how decorative or how skinny they are.

Yet we recognize that our bodies are God's creation, "fearfully and wonderfully made." We know and realize that body, mind, and spirit are closely interrelated. The way I exercise and eat and how I look can make a big difference in the ways that I feel and how I relate to others.

While I do not have to relent into the current obsession with a "beautiful body," I can make the most of God's work...

Beautiful Elation

Tremendous waves of passion forming deep within a lively soul,
Touching heartbreaking hearts and miraculously making them whole.
Radiant smiles blessing old and young,
Newfound wings spread open wide, forming a delightful life which has recently just begun.
Windows to the soul welcoming with sparkling and glittering crystal blue hues,
Keeping hearts locked up tight so the key he will never lose.
Tinkling giggles and laughter bring to this world a new song,
Heart beating for the passions of life with endless possibilities; who could ever go wrong?
Releasing positive auras all around;
Sublime joy and endless happiness can always be found.
Beauty innocently hidden within an angel's face.
Every heart he touches now holds for him a very special place.
When God created this little guy, He did it with endless love.
He saw that the world needed an angel and sent him down from above.
Ecstatic bliss unexpectedly erupts in your soul
As placed within your hand is his little hand to freely hold.

Amanda Perry

Kisses warm and filled with love land on rose-colored cheeks.
Moments like these make life worthwhile and amazingly complete.
In his embrace, waiting patiently to be found,
Undying love, adoring acceptance, and complete trust showers all of those around.
A yearning childlike faith
Sent to learn and grow here on earth by Heaven's saving grace…
A smile as bright as the shining sun,
Laughter that warms the soul when begun,
Endless joy from my soul now does radiate;
I will most definitely thank my Father in Heaven for blessing my life with my nephew, Camden, at the Heaven's most wondrous gates…

Spring

Longing for the warmth of the sun's passionate kiss,
Imagining the welcoming rays upon my skin, bringing to my very essence eternal bliss,
Longing for the calming fragrances of the earth's newborn flowers and blooms,
Imagining the freshly-painted petals of each and every flower artistically in my mind looms,
Longing for the symphony of all the earth's creation,
Imagining the joyous songs of endless birds chattering, bringing to my yearning soul stupendous elation,
Longing for the brilliantly glowing flashes of millions of fireflies,
Imagining the guiding light from sparkling orbs above in the clear twilight nights,
Longing for the sweet lullabies of the newly-awakened frogs,
Imagining purifying dreams that these lullabies now cause,
Longing endlessly for continuous warm, whispering winds,
Imagining dazzling dances from excitement filled leaves blowing on each and every trees limb,

Amanda Perry

Longing always for the fragrance of freshly-cut grass,
Imagining the cooling crispness that exfoliates the taste buds while slowly sipping from a tall and refreshing glass,
Longing for brilliantly-painted butterfly wings to stretch and take flight,
Imagining watching each individual one painting a rainbow as they flutter with all of their might,
Longing and imagining,
Imagining and longing,
Waiting patiently for spring to arrive so I feel human and imaging that to nature I will now be belonging…

Lineage Of Grace

"He's coming…" Mary said.
"Oh, Joseph, Jesus is coming," she whispered as her hand gently cradled her weary head.
What did he know about helping a woman bear a child?
Was there time to find a midwife? For as of now, Mary's pain seemed only mild.
He found a pitchfork near the entrance of the cave and spread straw in the stable near the back,
Then down off of the donkey he yanked his blanket from the bulging pack.
Kindling and firewood were stacked to one side of the cave and a cask of water stood near a trough; he tasted it and found it surprisingly fresh.
He then spread the blanket over the straw and helped Mary lie down: "While I build a fire, try to rest."
Within a few minutes, Joseph had a small fire going in the pit near the center of the cave.
Above it, the ceiling was blackened by years of soot, the floor caked with the packed dung of hundreds of animals who had been sheltered here over the year's passing days.

"I'm sorry, Mary," he knelt beside her, tears running down his cheeks into his beard.

"I'm so sorry I couldn't find a better place for him to be born," the pain coursing through to his heart seared.

She took his hand and pressed it against her flaming cheek, "God brought us here."

Her fingers tightened and she began to pant and groan as from her eyes fell giant pain-filled tears.

He begged God for wisdom, for help, for Mary's intense pain to be over, and for the child to be safely delivered.

And then, Mary uttered a sharp gasp, and Joseph saw water spread a stain over the blanket beneath her hips as with painful convulsions her body did quiver.

"Joseph, please go outside."

"But, Mary…" she was only fourteen, a mere child herself; how could she manage on her own?

His eyes filled with tears as he openly cried.

"Go, Joseph! Surely the Lord will guide me in this as he has guided us in everything thus far. Go, now."

She clenched her teeth, her shoulders rising from the ground. "Go! Now!"

Joseph obeyed and went outside, too tense to sit, he began to quickly pace.

Under his breath he began to pray; when he heard Mary moan, his heart did begin to race.

Chasms And Bridges Within The Heart

Staring up at the points of light in the dark sky; he sensed forces gathering around him as though invisible beings had come to witness this event;
Angelic or demonic, he didn't quite know yet.
Heart pounding and pulse racing, Joseph beseeched God for help and stepped back so that he was standing in the entrance of the cave.
The wind came up and, for an instant, he thought he heard laughter and a dark voice speaking: "Do you really believe you can protect them from me? Do you honestly believe that you are that brave?"
Joseph fell to his knees and raised his hands to the heavens,
Where God was upon His throne, and fervently he prayed,
"You are the Lord our God, the maker of the heavens and the earth.
Protect Mary and Your Son from the one who is trying to destroy them and take Your Son away."
And he stretched out his arms as though to take the full force of whatever would come against them.
The cold wind stopped completely and the air around him grew warm again.
His heart slowed as he heard the sound of wings and, suddenly, Scriptures flooded his mind: Don't be afraid, for I am with you... I am with you...
Mary uttered a last fierce cry as the Son of God slid from her body, bathed in water and blood and appearing purple, red, and blue.
Mary lifted him and held him against her breast, welcoming him into the world with soft joyous tears.
She was surprised that he, just like any other normal baby, did appear.
There was no hint of Shekinah glory or of the majesty of His Almighty Father.

Ten fingers, ten toes, a thatch of black hair, skinny little legs and arms and the wizened face of a newborn who had for nine long months dwelt in water.
She laughed as she wrapped him snugly in strip of cloth and held him again, kissing his face and cradling him tenderly in her arms,
"Jesus," she whispered, "My precious Jesus." She was filled with emotional alarm.
She held in her arms the hope of all Israel, the Anointed One of God, Son of Man, God the Son, the Son of God.
Closing her eyes, she breathed a little prayer: "Help me be his mother, Lord. Oh, please help me, God."
Mary rose on trembling legs, "Joseph," she called softly, "come and see Him."
Immediately, Joseph entered the cave, his face pale and sweating as though he had been the one in travail and not her;
she laughed softly in joy then.
Joseph came close and peered down at the baby, a look of surprise on his face.
Mary's knees were trembling with exhaustion, and she looked around for a warm, safe bed for her son; the safest place.
There was only the manger.
God would bless and protect this sweet baby from danger.
Mary stepped over and placed Jesus in the manger filled with straw.
When she turned, she felt extremely light-headed and feared a painful fall.
Joseph caught her up in his arms and placed her in a bed of fresh straw.
"I'm so sorry, my love," Joseph said in a chocked whisper.
"There's no one to help you but me… I am all."

Chasms And Bridges Within The Heart

Joseph rose and went to stand by the manger,
His heart beating fast he stared down at the tiny child stranger.
He touched the velvet soft skin of the infant's face and brushed the tiny palm.
When the baby's fingers closed around his finger, it was as if someone to his heart had rubbed a healing balm.
Never had he felt such encompassing joy- and spreading fear.
Am I to be his earthly father, Lord? A simple carpenter? Surely, Your Son deserves better than I!- he thought as in his eyes formed swelling tears.
The baby's eyes opened and looked up at him. Joseph's shame melted away as love filled him within. Leaning down, he kissed the tiny hand that gripped his finger.
Everything in him opened to the will of God, and God's power and love did begin to linger.
When footfalls sounded behind him, Joseph turned, sharply placing himself firmly in front of the manger,
Afraid for the safety of baby Jesus; afraid there may be danger.
An old shepherd stood at the entrance of the cave and a younger man just stood behind him.
They peered in with expressions of rapt curiosity:
"Is the child here," the older man stepped inside the cave. "The child of whom the angels spoke; the child of whom God did send?
"The angels?" Joseph saw many other shepherds behind these two and, beyond them, a flock of sheep in the grassland below the hillside cave.
"An angel of the Lord appeared among us, and the radiance of the Lord's glory surrounded us," the shepherds said as others crowded the entrance, "we were terrified, but the angel said not to be afraid."

Amanda Perry

The older shepherd looked from Joseph to Mary, asleep in the hay, then to the manager at the back of the cave, and his eyes twinkled with hope for the child that they sought.
"And this is how you will recognize him: you will find a baby lying in a manger, wrapped snuggly in strips of cloth!"
"Suddenly, the angel was joined by a vast host of others- the armies of heaven- praising God: 'Glory to God in the heaven, and peace on earth to all whom God favours.'"
"His name is Jesus," whispered Joseph and, as tears streamed down his face, he turned and gently lifted Jesus from the manger.
At the sound of Jesus' name, the shepherds fell to their knees with their faces aglow in the firelight.
"The Lord is come," the older shepherd said as Joseph closed his eyes and freely cried: "Blessed be the name of the Lord," and he held the baby tight.

Mary awakened in the wee hours of morning at Jesus' cry.
She drew him close and nursed him; marveling at what God had done for her, she smiled as she joyfully sighed.
When Jesus finished feeding, she rose carefully, wincing at the pain in her loins as she carried him back to the manger and snuggled him into the blanket cradled by hay.
Taking up her shawl, Mary went to the cave entrance and gazed up at the night sky which held a bright star that was shining as bright as day. It was like a shaft of glorifying light breaking through the floor of heaven and radiantly shining down on the City of David.

Chasms And Bridges Within The Heart

Had not Joel the prophet said the Lord would display wonders in the sky and on the earth when the Savior came, she silently wondered as her soul became elated.
Weariness swept over her and she turned away from the mouth of the cave.
Yawning, she returned to the bed that Joseph had so carefully made.

Outside, God's sentinels stood guard in the wild.
Finding no way to enter into the humble sanctum, Satan quickly sought different ways to destroy the child.
I will draw the traveling men off the track to Herod, for then my will shall be accomplished,
Dark laughter echoed in the night while this thought to his minions did Satan admonish.
The laughter, accompanied with howls of glee, through the night did slice.
The only person who was awakened and heard it was: Jesus the Christ…

Amanda Perry

Motherly Love

She never once gave up. My mom is my hero.
Kimberly Anne Brand,
Continuously radiating love most divine.
In her always open and welcoming arms can you find
A guardian angel sent from Heaven above.
She blesses your life and fills it with love;
A teacher, a sister, a friend.
When in need, she always provides for you a helping hand.
A tremendous strength she carries upon her shoulders.
A passion for life and love brightly and deeply within her eyes does smolder.
When life's storms around you rage, she's the shelter that hides you from the rain,
Always there to willingly listen and help you ease your pain.
She's the one who completes you, the one who indeed makes you whole,
The one to whom you owe your very life; the forming of your beautiful soul.
Always innocently making such sacrifices to always put you first.
Proudly and willingly she allows you to test your broken wings;
No matter how bad or how deeply it does hurt.

Chasms And Bridges Within The Heart

An amazingly talented artist who paints the world a rainbow
When it's filled with so many broken dreams.
She's capable of explaining it all so clearly when absolutely nothing at all is actually what it seems.
Sacrificing her own heart, her sweat, her tears,
Just to safely ensure that you make it successfully through each and every new year.
Yearning desires for God the Father she readily shares.
Not just for your physical well-being but also for your soul she does care.
When you feel like giving up because you feel all alone,
Her voice full of compassion, love, and understanding makes you feel at ease; makes you feel at home.
What way is there to thank you for changing with me as I changed;
Accepting all my flaws.
Not just loving me because you had to, but loving me *just because*.
For never even once giving up on me when your tortured wits had reached their end.
For always being proud of me and for being my very best friend.
Thank you for the endless gifts you freely give and everything you do.
But thank you, Mommy, most of all for making my dreams come true.

Amanda Perry

Martyrs

They are people that triumphantly wear the armor of God: the Helmet of Salvation, the Shield of Faith, and the Sword of God's Word. They face torture and death in their fight of faith, willing to stand for their beliefs and the Word of God, regardless of the price...

Written all throughout the greatest Book of all time, the Bible, are found multiple stories of great Christian Martyrs. They are stories of men and women who bravely and willingly stood up for their faith and trusted in the God of their Fathers; the God of Abraham, Isaac, and Jacob.

I'm sorry to those of you who enjoy reading my poetry, but this is not a poem. I was just reading in the Bible, and it occurred to me that there were a lot of Christ's own disciples and prophets who were martyred for His sake.

I can think of no other form of death that would be more fulfilling than being a martyr. Think about it for a minute...

To be able to stand up for God, to use your very last breath praising and glorifying God's Holy name, to show the world that God is indeed real and that nothing can stop the love of God for one of His precious children... I believe that there's no greater honour on this earth than to die a martyr for Christ Jesus.

Martyrdom is not just something that has happened in the past. It's happening now, as well. When we turn on the television, it's there... when we read our daily news, it's there... when we listen to our radios, it's there.

Chasms And Bridges Within The Heart

The Lord said that at the time of persecution, do not be afraid of what you must say because He will give you the words. He will fill your mouth and spirit with the Holy Ghost and will give you the words to use to bring Glory to His name.

Can you imagine that? Not using your own brain to think of things to say but, instead, just willingly opening up your mouth and hearing your voice as God uses it during your last hours to praise Him right in front of Satan and his demons!

People say that it's a horrible and gruesome way to die, but they're only looking at the physical act of the person who is dying. If you look at the spiritual side... and combine the physical act with it... I personally believe it's a very beautiful and peaceful way to die.

To know that at any minute you could be in Heaven standing alongside Jesus and knowing that as you were taking your last breath, you were still witnessing in His Glorious Name brings for me a sense of hopefulness... a sense of readiness.

Just some thoughts I have running through my head...

Amanda Perry

Ode To Rickie

My friend, Rickie, was definitely most amazing.
How I wish with my whole heart the world could see
Just how beautiful and loving he was;
How most compassionate he could be.
I wish I could just snap my fingers and bring Rickie back,
To hear and listen to his voice one last time; say words left unsaid.
I wish the world could see Rickie's true light shine-
Never bringing people down but building them up positively, instead.
I wish the world could share Rickie's radiant smiles
And the many amazing differences he did make,
Could see all the people his life had touched,
All of the difficult challenges he did take,
Noticed how he helped to make in his friend's lives a change.
Each and every day,
Helping us pass through life's major obstacles,
Guiding and helping us all along the narrow way.
I wish the world could come to realize
Exactly how tough and hard Rickie's life came to be.
All kinds of promises and dreams that were broken;
The hatred he did feel and see.

Chasms And Bridges Within The Heart

Yet still we must venture onward,
Unsure of where the road may lead,
Hoping the world will take notice,
Hoping they'll take heed
Of the changes that Rickie has made,
Of the power that he has come to behold,
Of the wisdom he has left unhidden,
Of the many stories that yet are untold.
I hope and pray the world will notice
What some of us have experienced and seen.
Rickie was the most amazing and one-of-a-kind person,
Who was always striving to do his best in helping
His friends to follow their dreams.

I wrote this poem for a wonderful friend, whom was taken to Heaven.
...we miss you, Rickie Cooper, and will never forget you. Rest in peace...

# Amanda Perry

Expressions Of Love

Shades of the color of grey dominate the vast expanse of endless skies.
The atmosphere is suffocating the sounds of nature; the ground slightly trembles where the waves of electric energy lies.
It seems as if the whole world has paused for a brief moment of time.
To some, this moment brings perverse pleasure, gladness, and even revenge; to others it brings sorrow, endless pain, a love not of this world but a love most divine.
In the storms of silence, a man greater than you and I endlessly suffers.
Upon His head is placed a crown of thorns; they pierce and tear into His flesh as He stands in the midst of the mockers and corruptors.
Serene calmness is the radiating aura all around Him.
The color of liquid red streams down His peaceful face; with each tearing of the flesh, the enemy believes it's his battle to win.
Never is one word spoken from His beautiful, cracked, swollen, and bloodstained lips.
The weapons of the highest degree of pain are chosen; showers of His blood run down His legs and form great running streams as piece after piece of skin opens and rips.

Chasms And Bridges Within The Heart

He is forced to listen to tumultuous applause and chorus after chorus of ecstatic glee.
In the distance comes a faint rumble of thunder; His body is badly broken and very weak as they place upon His shoulders the burden of His tree.
Faith never falters and love endless in His eyes remains with each step He takes.
His body falls to the ground and again is beaten; miraculously, He gets up and to the hill His journey makes.
White raiment stained, torn, and matted with blood from His body is stripped,
Thrown, and kicked down to His tree; sounds of flesh tearing and blood pouring as His skin on gentle hands and feet are severely ripped.
All around Him are deceivers and tempters as He gazes down at the crowd.
Father, forgive them; for they know not what they do; after He was given vinegar, these are His words spoken out loud.
Blackness fills the skies, and He can hear crying and endless weeping.
Father, into thy hands I commend my spirit; as a great earthquake rips the ground and temple as over the earth it goes sweeping…

Amanda Perry

The Answer That Can Only Be Found In Scripture

An immensely powerful army has now been formed.
I'm here to tell you about it and the evil deeds that they perform...
Coming into existence seemingly overnight.
To hear and see the evil they do fills you with frightful dreams and sleepless nights...
Their victims are the innocent and unsuspecting.
Christians are the people that for torturing they are collecting...
This vast army grows stronger with each passing day.
Their mission is simple: to rule, to dominate, to slay...
The Devil has been released from his lair.
His rule here on earth he has fiercely come to declare...
An evil and lurking darkness around this army does surround.
A strategy to defeat them just cannot be found...
Some say that we have absolutely nothing at all to fear.
I tell you, my friends, that they are already here...
It's just a matter of time
Until our own country will experience their insufferable crimes...

Chasms And Bridges Within The Heart

Brace yourself and be ready.
Make sure your faith is secure and steady...
They're coming...
They're coming...
Their footsteps march along to the Devil's sinister humming.
The Devil's own minions; they are insanely clever and cunning.
Defilement, destruction, and death they leave in their path.
What kind of power is being unleashed? The entire world will soon
experience it: the Devil's mighty and unrelenting wrath.
Walking among us, freely and calmly biding their time,
Pretending to be our friends while from their leader they patiently wait
for the sign...
The sign, the command, the order
To bring to this country chaotic disorder:

A usual and beautiful Sunday in church,
We prepare for fellowship and worshipping.
Blithely indulging in normal but uplifting routine,
Content... carefree... unaware...
A sudden and deafening blast startles us.
A car accident outside?
Deafening eruptions penetrate "Heavenly Father."
Sinuous and sinister voices now punctuated by gunshots, the demonic
splintering the angelic.
The fellowship quickly ceases
To the rhythmic beat of pounding hearts.
Fellow Christians scream throughout the sanctuary
As terror burns itself on innocent, God-seeking faces.
The aroma of burning and consuming smoke,
Innocent lives are forever changed.

Amanda Perry

Hysteria… Shock…
Why? What have we done?
The sound of bombs ignite, rushing horror through our veins
And send chills and severe trembling
That seems to puncture the skin like millions of needles.
Some try to run.
Some stand as a statue, paralyzed in shock,
Numbness engulfing all other feelings and all other emotions.
Swirling billows of a thick grey mist now blanket the sanctuary,
Developing and creating ghastly images.
I look through the delicate webs of swirling mists,
And I see the fruits of immense disgust and absolute hatred.
Bullets shatter glass
And invade precious bodies
As shear malice sears the souls of the perpetrators.
The preacher prays.
The choir director hides in stunned confusion.
A woman next to the altar bleeds.
Like little children,
We are helpless and horrified,
Longing for comfort and warming protection; longing to be in our mommy's arms.
Ceaseless screaming… bleeding corpses…
Why? What have we done?
Several faces,
Hidden under black turbans and masks reveal only eyes, appear through immense clouds of endless smoke.
The gruesome horror and calculating hatred strips away my consciousness.
My own first instinct is to run.

Chasms And Bridges Within The Heart

I duck my head as a gleaming massive blade slices through the smoky air.
Our church, God's Holy House, is now the grounds of insufferable warfare-
Mortal fighting
In a field of flaming fire, bullets, and slicing swords.
Weapons that have freely fallen into the wrong hands
Have but one single purpose, and they
Are killing us, and all I hear is angered shouts of a foreign language
And mass weapons of destruction.
Crackling, bursting,
Ringing, crackling, humming, chilling screaming, what now, Lord?
Too much to handle
Too soon to die
Too young to see
So scared, so horrified, so sick
Help us… Lord God in Heaven, please help us…
I struggle to escape but am slowed
As if sinking in quicksand.
Through the shattered windows, I see fiery flames and immensely darkening smoke that completely absorb the sky and sun.
I see nothing now inside but shear blackness.
I can no longer freely breathe; as more screams of agony erupt and prayers are boldly stated, I'm suffocating.
I am almost lost in oblivion.
Footsteps stop right beside me.
The sharpened blade gently runs across my exposed and sweating neck,
Creating chills and the necessity to proclaim my love and my very life for my one and only true God, Jesus Christ.
Laughter as the blade slices through skin…

Amanda Perry

Blackness, silence…

There is a House of God
Where countless broken and burned bodies lie
And where others by the flames are being consumed.
In the darkness of the smoke-filled sanctuary,
Heaven's angels embrace the lifeless,
And their wings flicker sparkling light
Against a wall of darkened shadows.
God now wraps His arms
Around the burning church
And gathers the souls of His children,
Makes strong the souls of the weak,
Cries for the violence on this beautiful Earth.

Time continues passing and the Devil's army grows stronger, larger, undefeatable.
Our world is being destroyed,
And God's people are being separated and scattered.
Why? What have we done?
This answer can only be found in Scripture…

Interacting With The Author

The Word of God is living and active. **(Hebrews 4:12)**

There is a book that is alive and breathing.
This book is most definitely well worth reading.
When reading this book, the Author is always with you.
It contains the power to change, enlighten, and renew.
In its pages you can find: mystery, action, and romance.
It's always there to comfort you, no matter what your circumstance.
Looking for answers to unsolvable problems in your life?
Looking for relief from constant pain and ongoing strife?
Seeking a friend and loyal companion who truly understands?
Seeking a better life and need an uplifting hand?
Yearning for acceptance and everlasting guidance?
Yearning for an escape from the world's ceaseless fighting and endless violence?
Needing a relationship built truly on unconditional love?
Needing to satisfy a burning curiosity about Heaven and the Man above?
While reading this book, within its golden-trimmed pages, you will find
An Author with the most divinely appointed and caring mind,
An Author whose words are very true and always reliable.
This Author is God and His book?
His Book is titled: The Holy Bible…

Since God is personally present when we receive His answers from the Bible, it is most logical that He expects us to interact with Him about what He has said. Since this is the only Book in which the Author is always present while it is being read, it is also true that this is the only Book where a personal interaction with the Author, God, is necessary.

The Bible is different from all other books ever written because it is truly alive:

> For the Word of God is quick, and powerful, and sharper than any two edged sword, piercing even to the dividing asunder of soul and spirit, and of the joints and marrow, and is a discerner of the thoughts and intents of the heart.
> **(Hebrews 4:12)**

This, I believe, is only possible because God Himself, its Author, is active in its convicting, enlightening, and instructing process. Therefore, the Bible can be applied practically only through spiritual involvement with God Himself, and this amazing interaction is called prayer.

We must respond personally to God about what He has said to us-asking forgiveness for that specific sin, staying quietly in His Holy presence while He cleanses us, seeing ourselves in contrast to His divine holiness, imploring Him to make us more like the Jesus He just showed us.

There is no other author who discerns and judges the thoughts and the intents of our hearts and scrutinizes the spiritual, emotional, and intellectual aspects of our lives. Nor do we stand before any other author stripped bare and fully exposed, with nothing concealed. **(Hebrews 4:13)**

Therefore, no other book consistently and without fail can have prerecorded answers for the immediate and specific needs of the reader, for no other author is actively involved in the inmost and hidden self of the reader...

Thank You, Lord,
For Your beautiful Book of everlasting truth and wisdom. Thank You for supplying Your children with this Book throughout all the ages of this world. It, indeed, is a comfort to those who use It. It, indeed, contains all the answers to our endless questions about this life and the hereafter. Thank You,
Amen

Amanda Perry

The First Blush Of Spring

In a magical valley, way beyond the clouds,
Lies a beautiful place that the rainbow shrouds.
Spring it always stays;
Glorious and perfect here are the days.
This magical valley is home to millions of tiny fairies.
Each fairy is important; each one has a task which it carries.
The Earth relies on these magical and mystical fairies to bring every year a beautiful Spring.
To bring happiness to the people, that makes their hearts sing.
Wind fairies use their soft tinkling wings to bring whispers to the blowing wind.
Warm and slightly-scented breezes their fluttering wings do send.
Lovingly and gently they caress each newborn leaf.
Bringing to all of nature from the heat of the sun, cooling relief.
Water fairies release magical power that thaws the ice coated over streams, lakes, and rivers.
Beautiful lullabies they bring to life with the trickling and babbling waters they deliver.
Rejuvenating and refreshing rain showers they do create.

Chasms And Bridges Within The Heart

Sparkling drops of glistening dew for the Earth's early mornings they do make.
Light fairies use their glistening wings to catch tiny rays of radiant light shining from the sun.
They radiate the sun's great warmth to melt the winter away and to let people know that Spring has begun,
Thawing the frozen Earth.
Each flower's seed and each frozen plant the light fairies gently and readily unearth.
Animal fairies use their magical powers to awaken winter's precious sleeping beauties.
Mystical and heavenly voices along with tinkling wings are used to perform these miraculous duties.
Dazzling, musical fairy dust they proudly sprinkle upon the Earth,
Filling all animals, people, and especially birds with whimsical and musical mirth.
Rainbow fairies are extremely beautiful and full of multicolored grace.
Their wings flutter a colorful arch of sparkling powder upon the Earth's face.
Their favourite time to take flight is right after a Spring shower.
The Earth stands in appreciated awe of the radiant rainbow's vibrant power.
The rosebud fairies are very special, indeed.
Their magic brings forth vibrant, colored petals which lay sleeping in tiny seeds.
Intoxicating fragrances are born within their fluttering rose-colored wings.
Working together, these fairies paint a most dazzling masterpiece:
The First Blush of Spring!

Amanda Perry

The Empty Tomb

He is not here: for He is risen, As he said. Come, see the place where The Lord lay. **(Matthew 28:6)**

Darkening and billowing clouds quickly begin swirling and rolling in;
So dark that the day has become completely dim.
Great drops of much-needed rain begins to fall from the ever-darkening, ominous skies.
The whole world sits in stunned silence and, for the Man upon the cross, silently and mournfully begins to cry.
His perfect body now hangs limp and steaming from the cooling rain upon the immense cross.
My body shudders in great convulsions as uncontrollable tears fall from my eyes; I slowly realize that our Savior to the darkness of death we have forever lost.
I bow my head and somehow find the strength I need to pray.
The ground I'm kneeling on suddenly trembles and feels as if it will soon give way.
Frightened screams erupt as people are knocked to the ground off of their feet.
All around the city, houses begin to shake and crumble, even those built from brick and thickly strong concrete.
Great wailing and intensely terrifying shrieks rise up from around the Temple as it begins to shake.

Chasms And Bridges Within The Heart

A severe ripping and tearing sound reaches my ears as the Temple's veil is rent in two from the fierceness of the sudden and great earthquake.

Panic-stricken people are running to unknown destinations.

Giant boulders splitting in half and violently crashing to the ground make it seem as if being destroyed is God's wondrous creation.

Rocks, which are the guardians of the sealed tombs, crack and crumble to the shaking earth.

Once-sealed graves of many wondrous saints are suddenly unearthed.

I find myself staring in sheer awe and wonder as these saints appear alive and actually breathing.

Each one of them begins walking toward the Holy City as if they have a command to follow; appearing too many and with their teaching the people they truly begin reaching.

My gaze fell upon the centurion and his many people who are watching Jesus with amazement and awesome awe.

They began trembling and crying out in unison: "Truly, this was the Son of God."

Tears keep falling from my swollen, red-rimmed eyes.

I see a group of women gathering at the foot of the cross and hear their mournful wailing and grief-filled cries…

A woman kneels upon the muddy earth, gazing into the beautiful face of her Beloved Son.

His face was already cold from the rain that to her skin violently stung.

Slowly and gently, she began removing the crown of thorns from upon His precious head.

She shuddered and gasped for breath as sharpened thorns, momentarily embedded, began to rip and slice open fresh new wounds which violently poured and bled.

Her heart ached with endless pain

As she watched the fresh blood wash away with the showers of the rain.

Amanda Perry

She cradled His face against her trembling shoulder and silently muttered a prayer.
At that moment, Joseph of Arimathaea, came to gently collect Jesus' body, and in his own newly-sculptured tomb, he was to bury the Savior there.
When Joseph had brought the body of Jesus to the tomb which he had prepared for just this reason,
He gently bathed the body and dried it clean, erasing all signs of mud and dry, cracking bleeding.
He had in a sack in the corner, a clean and white linen cloth.
He took his time wrapping the precious body as his mind wandered over memories never to be lost.
He rolled a great stone to the door of the tomb and slowly departed.
Tomorrow would be a day that would very wearily for him get started…
The next day, which was the day after the preparation, the chief priests and Pharisees came together and went before Pilate.
They were troubled for they remembered what Jesus had said and thought Him still a great deceiver and still possibly violent:
"After three days, I will rise again."
They commanded that the tomb be sealed shut tightly so that Jesus' body could not be taken and hidden by some of His followers and friends.
So the tomb was sealed and a watch was set.
Now, no longer would the Pharisees and priests continue to fret…
Very early in the morning of the first day of the week,
Mary Magdalene and Mary, the mother of James and Salome, had brought sweet spices, and to the tomb they journeyed together, anointing Jesus is what they did seek.
The two women stopped suddenly and gazed at one another in fear.
Beneath their feet, the earth violently trembled and to each other for protection they did quickly draw near.

Chasms And Bridges Within The Heart

A sudden burst of blinding light parted the clouds and illuminated all around the tomb.
The two women slowly backed away, their hearts filling with fear and impending doom.
Born from the radiant, pulsing light descended an Angel from Heaven.
Frozen with fear, the women could only hope for rescue and help from their brethren.
The Angel of the Lord came gently down and rolled back the stone from the entrance of the tomb and patiently sat upon it.
His raiment was as pure and as white as snow, and His countenance was like lightning and was dazzlingly lit.
The keepers of the tomb violently and uncontrollably did shake.
When their eyes beheld the glorious Angel, they all fell upon the ground, their lives it appeared the Angel did take.
The Angel turned and faced the two women;
The light continued to keep his face well hidden.
His voice was beautiful, awakening all senses and filling the women with happiness and hope.
It was commanding yet melodious as he spoke:
"Fear not ye: for I know that ye seek Jesus, which was crucified; He is not here: for He is risen, as He said. Come, see the place where the Lord lay."
"And go quickly, and tell His disciples that He is risen from the dead; and, behold, He goeth before you into Galilee; there shall ye see Him: lo, I have told you."
The women ran away quickly from the empty tomb with fear and tremendous joy,
They became worried that the disciples would only believe their words as a great false ploy.
As the women were leaving the country, they heard the words: "All hail"
They both looked and before them stood Jesus, their hearts did almost fail!

Amanda Perry

Both of the women fell at His beautiful, scarred feet,
Joyously worshipping Him, to say His name aloud was most amazingly sweet.
"Be not afraid: go tell my brethren that they go into Galilee, and there shall they see me…"
He was beautiful and real and amazingly alive.
God was faithful and true; His Son was not dead forever, but forever He would always thrive.
A light, a brilliant warm glow radiated from deep within.
The scars on His hands and feet were real to the touch, were truly there forever placed upon His skin.
His voice breathed wisdom and undying love.
As He spoke to them all while lifting His hands to His Father above:
"All power is given unto Me in Heaven and in earth."
"Go ye therefore, and teach all nations, baptizing them in the name of the Father, and of the Son, and of the Holy Ghost:"
"Teaching them to observe all things whatsoever I have commanded you: and, lo, I am with you always, even unto the end of the world.
Amen.

Control

From the moment we are conceived, we find ourselves desperately fighting for life;
A life full of hatred, rage, murder, and endless strife.
As we grow and age, day by day,
So do our battles all along our life's narrow way…

A young woman into her pillow cries every night.
Every day, she wakes up and seriously wonders if her life is well worth the fight.
She finds herself confused and very alone,
Often longing for acceptance and a loving and welcoming home.
Violently torn away from her childhood,
She's witnessed things that, to you, can never be understood.
She has been forced to suffer in silence
The act of brutal domestic violence.
It's followed her all throughout the years.
She has well hidden the pain and stifled the fears.
Watching as her mother tried to fight her stepfather away,
Hearing the screaming, the crying, the fighting as she and her younger sister were told to go play.

Amanda Perry

Broken and cracked ribs, swollen black eyes, and bloodstained busted lips;
Through all of this, yet, her mother to this man still commits.
She greedily reads endless amounts of books.
Away from her nightmare of reality each book gently her mind took.
She was the one who showed comfort to her younger siblings.
She was forced to be the strong one, the one to hide all of her feelings.
She withdrew into herself and became sullen and quiet.
All the while emotions inside of her raged, causing a chaotic riot.
Kids her age never could understand her.
A life of solitude she lived; for her depression there was no cure.
A life swirling in rivers of insufferable pain.
A life where, each and every day, the sun was blocked by massive dark clouds pouring; always pouring the rain.
Things never got better; they most certainly got worse.
The abuse was no longer aimed at her mother, but instead it became reversed.
This man, so full of anger and hate,
Took away her child-like innocence in the violent act of rape.
Her world came crashing down all around her.
She fought for control, the need for it deeply within her stirred.
So, she controlled what she could.
She found she could make herself skinny while at the same time punish herself for the rape, and she honestly felt that she should.
Thus began her ongoing fight with Bulimia and endless depression.
When at first she lost the weight, she felt and looked terrific, of that there's no question.

Chasms And Bridges Within The Heart

That was just the perk of the deadly controlling addiction.
She became elated with this newly-found control; within her being, it created a great and fiery friction.
The pain and misery of her life was no longer a burden upon her shoulders.
Her passions for life became reborn and even more bold for her.
Years and years quickly passed by.
During all that time, she had been living just to die…

Amanda Perry

The Beauty Of A Mother's Expecting

A brilliance of endless beauty radiating deeply within the soul,
Breathes magnificent sparkling beams of light that pulsate all around the aura, making personality aglow.
Like a babbling brook, sweet ecstasy of delight bubbles up from deep within,
Filling glittering currents of expectation and happiness to the depths of a longing soul up and over the ever-widening brim.
On glistening jewels of the radiance of the rainbow, a heart finds its wings and fluttering does begin to take flight.
Each gentle stroke of the wings brings precious life into a miraculous masterpiece, divinely pleasing the sight.
Euphoric sensations swirling and enveloping lost and carefully hidden emotions.
Giving birth to dazzling radiance of a guardian's protection and a most motherly devotion.
Soft and gentle little nudges bloom and blossom within warm and serene hopes and dreams.
Beautifully innocent newfound life developing within splashing, loving, vibrant, colorful gleams.
Ribbons of pure and uplifting inspirations engulf many multiple inspiring future aspirations.

Chasms And Bridges Within The Heart

Limitless, majestic, glorifying sparkles decorate a Heavenly portrait of God's endless creations.
Beautiful rhythms bringing a heart-warming symphony, provoking glistening tears.
Dancing prisms of a diamond's radiance filters light through the many upcoming mysterious years.
Angels from Heaven descending with God's blessing gifts from above,
Appointedly surround the essence within, showering blissful drops of unconditional, everlasting love.
Enlightening realizations being born upon clouds of defining bliss,
Awaiting the precious moment of sharing our newborn first kiss!

Amanda Perry

Exaltations From My Soul

Majestic praise and honour do I give to the Lord on High.
His mercy radiates through the beauty of the heavens, giving my broken heart majestic wings and soaring to the Lord of my salvation it does fly.
His faithfulness falls from the clouds,
Showering sparkles of promising life and love, around my soul it protectively shrouds.

Majestic praise and honour do I give to the Lord on High.
His righteousness creates the great mountains upon this Earth, and trembling with blazing worship they to the God of Heaven cry.
His love is excellent and, like the depths of the raging ocean, it engulfs me in the deep,
Permitting my soul to trust and flourishing thrive with the promises that His love does keep.

Majestic praise and honour do I give to the Lord on High.
My soul has become abundantly satisfied with the drink from the river of His pleasures and gratefully does sigh.
In the God of Heaven, I have found the everlasting fountain of life.
Great rejoicing within my soul erupts, for I will be blessed in Heaven from all of my earthly persecutions and strife.

Chasms And Bridges Within The Heart

Majestic praise and honour do I give to the Lord on High.
My tongue blissfully exalts His righteousness and, glorifying Him all the day long, wondrous prayers do arise.
Evening, morning, and at noon will the God of Heaven hear my calling voice.
His mercy has delivered my everlasting soul in eternal peace from the raging battle that was against me by my own free will of choice.

Majestic praise and honour do I give to the Lord on High.
My trust have I completely surrendered to Him, nevermore fearing how and when my body shall die.
His promising vows are placed protectively upon me,
Delivering my soul from eternal damnation will I forever continue to believe and to see.

Majestic praise and honour do I give to the Lord on High.
Upon His rock of salvation and endless truth does my very soul rely.
His mercies and blessings are better than life itself,
The God of Heaven is my help and in the shadow of His sheltering wings no greater love have I ever felt.

Majestic praise and honour do I give to the Lord on High.
Gladly He has received me, my Father; no child He will ever deny.
A father of the fatherless, God has blessed me with sustaining strength.
In the God of Heaven am I no longer lost; my life has finally found the missing link.

Amanda Perry

Majestic praise and honour do I give to the Lord on High.
To Him that rideth upon the heavens of heavens who sends out His great voice which thunders from the sky.
He is clothed with majesty and great strength that will always last forever,
A relationship with the God of Heaven carries an eternal bond that absolutely no evil can or ever will be able to sever.

Majestic praise and honour do I give to the Lord on High.
Let us sing to the God of Heaven a new and glorious song, come and let us make a joyful noise, together; let us together comply.
In His wondrous hands, He cradles gently the whole world, His entire creation.
Let us worship and bow down: let us kneel before the Lord and gallantly send our oblations.
For the Lord is great, and worthy is He to be praised.
Great honour and majesty are always before Him;
Because of Him is my very soul ablaze!

Majestic praise and honour do I give to the Lord on High.
Great and terrible is His wondrous name, and I will praise it by and by.
I will willingly serve the God of Heaven with gladness and will dance before His Presence with singing.
I will enter into His gates with thanksgiving and into His courts with praise; the echo of my voice will joyfully be ringing…
Majestic praise and honour do I give to the Lord on High!

Violent Forcing From Childhood

I lay in bed, holding my younger sister very protectively tight.
I turn the radio on and volume up, hoping to drown out the screaming and the fight.
My sister trembles in my embrace from uncontrollable, falling tears.
Countless nights just like this have we spent over the past few years.
I silently wait for my sister to fall into a troubled slumber.
Then, I can release my emotions; torrents of hysterical sobs washing over my body like a river, making me feel as if I'm going under.
Closing my eyes, I quietly sing alone to the radios song,
Wishing with my whole heart that to this kind of life my sister and I did not belong.
Violent screaming and obscene language broke through the playing music and interrupted my thoughts.
My heart raced as my sister covered her ears and my stomach tightened into uncomfortable giant knots.
Fearing for our mommy's safety was always on our minds.
He was always fighting with her, physically hurting her I don't even know how many times.

Amanda Perry

Loud and thundering footsteps sounded in the hall.
As if he has started chasing her, I cringe as I await the horrible sound of her defeating fall…
The sound is muffled as he wraps his hands around her throat and pushes her down to the floor.
I realize that my mom, well, she's a strong woman; she never gives up even though the abuse comes frequently more and more.
Everything becomes quiet as suddenly the fighting stops.
In a drunken stupor, he has finally to the couch let his body drop.
A little while later, mommy comes in and carefully lays down with us on our bed.
My sister and I pretend that we're already asleep with pleasant dreams playing in our heads…
A few more years slowly pass on by.
Still nothing has changed; abuse and fear still rule the life of our mom, my sister, and I.
Love?
The reason she stayed with him was love.
The drinking never stopped; it only became worse.
I truly began to believe that my sister and I had at birth been cursed.
He started staying out late at his friend's places and at bars.
Our mom would go looking for him with my sister and I in the backseat of the car.
We found him one rainy summer night at an old country bar.
They began fighting outside, and he grabbed mom's shirt collar, ripping it as he slammed her back against the wet windshield of the car.

Chasms And Bridges Within The Heart

Filling with fear, my sister cried out for: "Mommy!"
"Mom!"
Jerking the car door open and leaning into the backseat, he bellowed:
"Shut up and stop crying! Hold your tongue!"
Terrified he would hurt my sister and I, my arms wrapped her shoulders
as we both began to violently cry.
The only thought running through my mind was why?
Why…?
Our family was falling apart.
Depression quickly sets in and ways to cope running through our minds
does begin to start.
Ways to release the pain;
Ways to keep from going insane,
Believing it was all our fault and our own doing,
Ways to punish ourselves, we each began persuing.
Cutting…
Something about seeing the blood drip from the fresh cut brought
relief.
Maybe, it was seeing mommy get hurt that made us think we needed to
hurt also is what I personally have come to believe.
For me, cutting only helped a little; it just wasn't enough.
I was forced to witness abuse, to comfort my sister, stepbrother, and
sometimes even my cousin. Our grandpa, who I was very close to, had
died right before things began to get worse; my childhood was taken
away and my life was very tough.
What can you do when you have no control?
What will make you feel better? Make you feel whole?
Anorexia… Starvation…

Amanda Perry

I could control and punish myself at the same time; at first it brought constant elation.
Then, I found I couldn't stand the feeling of always being hungry; I had to eat.
So, I just went back to watching the cycles of domestic violence repeat and repeat...
Then came the day when the pattern unexpectedly changed.
Something was way off and just not right; mom started sleeping a lot all through the night, which she never did before; it was actually very strange.
That's when it happened to me.
While he was raping me, he hit me so I would keep quiet, you see.
Again, depression.
Again the control obsession.
Bulimia... Binge Eating...
When I threw up, I imagined it was what he had done inside of me that I was releasing.
I had control of something in my life.
I could ease some of the pain and ease some of the strife.
Losing weight was a wonderful bonus and brought such happiness.
To slowly regain control in my life was now effortless.

Please know that before you judge someone struggling with a disorder, whether it be eating disorders, drug addictions, prescribed medications- that there's probably a reason why they do what they do. Sometimes, it's just for kicks and fun, but most likely, it's from something that has happened in that person's life. They're looking for a way to escape, a way to feel normal and accepted, trying to regain control of a life that was by someone else brutally destroyed.

So, please, don't be so quick to judge someone else. It's not our place to do that, nor our job. People struggling with disorders and addictions don't need to feel hated or singled out. They need to be shown love, acceptance, and guidance and trust. They need to know that there's hope and that, with time, things will get better.

Yes, I am a recovering bulimic, and yes, I still have bad days; extremely hard and tough bad days. But there's always someone there for you: friends, family, and most importantly God. God does not care about the things you have or are doing. He loves you, He accepts you for you, and He uses these people with disorders to reach out and help others that are suffering.

When all hope seems lost, reach out to God. He's there, you know, with open arms and endless showers of love. He wants to help you, to heal you, and to save you. Give it to God. Talk with Him about it. I guarantee you will see things in a new light. Your life will change for the best.

Of course, you will still be reminded of your disorder or addiction, but that's just Satan working his ways. I sometimes have a relapse and find myself throwing up, but I now feel severely awful and guilty when I do. That's when I immediately go straight to God and talk with Him about it. He understands. We are not perfect; we are all human. We make mistakes and He understands and still loves and forgives us.

My relapses have become less and less, thanks to God, my amazing family, and awesome friends. I have a purpose and that's to share my story and help people as much as I possibly can. I work for the Lord and He will bless me in Heaven. There is help… There is hope… There is love… There is life… There is forgiveness… and There is a cure…

Amanda Perry

A Remembered Place

I remember a place that beautifully haunts my dreams;
A place always most welcoming and loving; a place that seems to glitter and to my own eyes to gleam.
A place way out in the West Virginia country, surrounded by the vast rolling hills,
Lies a most beautiful place that warming comfort and endless love into the depths of your soul joyously fills.
An old dirt road surrounded by acres and acres of richly thriving farm land;
A most artistically painted masterpiece created by God's most glorious hands.
Our Creator was permitting us a glimpse into His own breathtaking Promise Lands.
Fluffy, white, and billowing marshmallow clouds gently roll across the open and endless beautiful blue skies.
Whispering breezes warm the soul and swirling fragrant winds throughout this land lazily glides.
Never has another place been blessed with such vibrant color, continuous seasons of endless beauty, and earthly fragrances of nature's creation.
This place is a place of peaceful rest, a place of the soul's healing, a place worthy of the Lord's dedication.

Chasms And Bridges Within The Heart

The whispers of the wind
Are the carriers of the whispered promises that to this place God does continually send.
The twittering of the birds' jubilant and peaceful songs
Are the welcoming instruments that keep calling to your soul, reminding you that here, to this place, you do truly belong.
The babbling trickles of the cooling streams
Are the peaceful lullabies that at night to your heart quietly sings.
The gentle swaying of the tall slender grass
Let you know that the memories of this place will never die but will always and forever last.
The intoxicating fragrance of the earth's rich soil
Shows that hard work pays off and bountiful gardens right before your very eyes begin to unfoil.
Upon a hill, overlooking this beautiful place,
Lies the eternal slumbering of the past generations; angels of Heaven who are its guardians, divinely sent from Grace.
This land and place was their life, their inspiration, their own glorious treasure.
To be laid at rest here, I believe, is from God the greatest of pleasures.
Upon this land and place they built for themselves a warm and happy home.
They worked and cultivated this land, knowing that to this place they would always belong.
I believe that this place is truly the closest that we'll ever get to Heaven upon Earth.
Memories of this beautiful place truly fill your heart with longing and great mirth…

Amanda Perry

I remember a woman who once lived at this place.
Her home was always open with her there to greet you with a big growing and warming smile upon her face.
Her voice always soft and gentle;
Her hugs and kisses always generous and plentiful;
Her long and flowing white hair she neatly kept pulled back and up in a bun.
How I loved coming here as a child! I always had such wondrous fun!
Her kitchen was always very busy but kept very clean.
A woman with immense strength and determination could always be seen.
Her kitchen table was always bountiful with home-cooked food.
The aromas of her cooking wafting throughout the house was always sure to improve any mood.
A very hard working woman she was and very beautiful, too.
I always thought she was prettiest wearing my two favourite colors of different shades of pink and different hues of light blue.
I remember a man who once lived at this place,
Farming was in his blood; it was what made his heart race.
He enjoyed teaching the younger generations his farming ways.
He had a strong voice and countenance that to this very day, with me, stays.
God used this man to make this place what it is today;
A beautiful piece of Heaven I hope and pray it will always stay.
This man was always strong-willed and dedicated to his family.
A man like him, on this earth, will there never be.
He used his own two hands
To make a home and life upon this magnificent land.

Chasms And Bridges Within The Heart

He was loved by many and very well respected.
When you wanted a hug from him, you were never rejected.
He loved to make the children laugh by telling his jokes.
Providing for his family and keeping this place beautiful his life he did devote…

This is dedicated to my great grandma and my great grandpa:
Ona Bell and Alvin Perry. May their memories live on and never be forgotten.
Rest in peace with our Father in Heaven.
I will always remember you and miss you.
Love you,
Amanda Perry

Amanda Perry

Angel Of Light

Flying?…
Floating?…
Dying?…
This did not seem like a dream.
I felt weightless, drifting higher and higher, my head spinning as around me the world began to careen.
Despite this incredible lightness of being, I felt as conscious and aware as I had ever been.
I began to wonder if maybe I was dying again.
My senses had never felt so alive.
I could see clearly and feel everything from temperature to the static-filled air moving over the hair on my arms as onward and upward I continued to glide.
I could hear every sound in the darkening night, from frogs croaking to the whistling wind.
Gliding higher and higher, I felt euphoric and blissful of the feeling of flying that gliding did send.
The new and fresh spring air was cool and crisp above the shrinking houses and trees.
Yet I was extremely glad and grateful that I was wearing long shirtsleeves.
It was no way near uncomfortable, but I was extremely aware of everything… feeling, hearing, seeing
The wind through the bare-leafed trees gently breezing.

Chasms And Bridges Within The Heart

The house, the road, the cars, and buildings became minuscule beneath me.
Would I grow colder soon, would all oxygen quickly away from me flee?
How was it even possible that I was already this far from home so soon,
Looking now at a beautiful blue glowing globe illuminated by a marvelously shining moon?
I felt as if I were gliding in the endlessly deep recesses of space.
I looked around and all I saw were blazing stars and immense swirling galaxies which made my heart race.
I reached for the earth, because it was receding way too quickly.
I felt strange, my entire body tangled and the hairs on my arms suddenly felt prickly.
I was able to see the breathtaking planets as I continued drifting, drifting, drifting…
How fast could I possibly be going?…
How far up was I gradually lifting?…
Where was I and where exactly was I going?
It was so strange, so wonderfully amazing, so mind blowing.
As I seemed to hang weightless in space, it seemed as if I began to accelerate, yet again,
Racing through the vast universe with its numerous galaxies and breathtaking solar systems.
The only sounds I could hear were my heartbeat and my own rhythmic breathing,
Which was peaceful and deep, as if I were truly sleeping.
How could my human mind create such a dream?
Suddenly, the darkness turned to the brightest light, obliterating the total darkness of space with its radiant beam.
Everything into this glorious light disappeared.
This light, so powerful that it could destroy a shadow, surrounded me from behind and I trembled with fear.
Trembled with fear from again seeing darkness,

Amanda Perry

I welcomed the light, it seemed to actually beckon me, to will me to turn around and face the brilliant brightness.
And no longer controlling my body, turn I did…
I felt such a wondrous sense of peace and safety that I did not want this to end, dream or not.
As my eyes adjusted to the light, I could make out a man's immense figure which was huge and bright and strong, but as it should have been frightening to me, well, it most definitely was not.
The man had a massive beard that framed a face that appeared kindly and yet not soft, loving and yet very confident and firm.
This was the most sensory-rich experience of my life that I could ever possibly learn.
My voice almost failed me but came out shaky and incredibly high,
"Are you Jesus the Son of God?"
"Are you Jesus the Christ?"
"No," came a gentle and kind voice that seemed to surround me.
"No, daughter of the earth, it is only one of His princes that before you you do see."
"Michael is my name."
Questions burned inside me, igniting my soul like a burning flame.
"Prince of the living God, have I died?"
"Your time has yet to come," he softly chuckled the reply.
"Why am I here if I am not indeed dead?"
"You have much to learn, and the Father does bless your hand; the people need to hear and need to understand," he finally said.
"Please, teach me all I am here to learn."
"My soul and mind are ready; my heart for this knowledge does yearn."
"Stand still, stand silent," the Angel said.
"Observe, and give ear to the truth of the war in Heaven.
Since the calling up of the righteous dead and alive, the enemy has competed with the hosts of Heaven for the remaining souls of men," he softly said.

Chasms And Bridges Within The Heart

"That old serpent, the evil one, has had access to the throne of the Most High since the beginning of time, until now, the appointed time."
What was it that this angel to me was trying to imply?
I looked passed the Angel Michael into the very throne room.
I saw only one figure there that right in front of me did loom.
Much bigger than Michael, more beautiful, and more bright.
"Is it the Lamb of God? Is it Jesus the Christ?" I tried with the angel to confer.
"Silence, daughter of the earth. This is neither Son nor Father, but before you is the angel of light, the beautiful star, the great deceiver, Lucifer."
I violently shuddered, disgusted, and yet unable to look away.
"Listen and learn," the angel Michael did say.
I was suddenly able to hear the other beautiful angel plead his case before the throne.
"Your children are beneath you, ruler of Heaven," came the very persuasive tones.
"Give them to me, and I will create a force unlike any army that you have ever seen."
From the hidden throne came a voice of such power and great authority that throughout the Heavens it screamed:
"Thou shalt not touch my beloved children!"
"But I shall ascend to a throne higher and more glorious than Yours with them!"
"No!"
"They are too weak and ineffective in Your service; You will never win!"
"No!"
"Give me these children or I will-"
"No."
"I will-"
"Thou shalt not!"

Amanda Perry

"I will destroy them all and will defeat You! I shall sit high above the Heavens, and there shall never be no God like me!"

"God, the eternal Father Almighty," Michael shouted, causing the angry evil one to look his way and to him finally see.

"Allow no more of his blasphemy in Heaven! Grant that I destroy this evil one and cast him out and away from Your sight!"

Lucifer glared with contempt at Michael, smirking and laughing, enjoying the fight.

"Michael… Michael… Michael, your Master shall not grant you an impossible task! He knows I am right about the sons of God. In my light they shall bask!"

As I watched and listened, Lucifer's voice began to change.

It became very high-pitched and extremely whiny; it sounded slithery and completely strange.

As he pleaded, challenged, and begged, the voice from the throne still continued to deny him, making his face fluster.

Suddenly his brightly sparkling robe lost all of its light and all of its luster.

The skin on his face melted away and revealed a hideous mask of slimy scales.

His hands and feet completely disappeared, and his robe to the floor fell.

Before me was an enormous slimy, writhing, and coiling hideous serpent.

Slithering around as if he was caught in the raging river's current. His voice became a violent stinging hiss.

Then a thunderous roar as he transformed himself; I stared in frozen terror completely and utterly transfixed.

My body shuddered and my insides cringed as his hands and feet reappeared.

His fingers and toes turned into great sharpened horned appendages that were a magnificent white that glittered.

He dropped to all fours and paced before the throne.

Chasms And Bridges Within The Heart

His words became flaming breaths and thunderous guttural tones.
His head sprouted great sharpened horns and a crown sat upon it, sparkling and polished pure gold.
From blackened and green scales, his entire body became a fiery vibrant red.
As I watched in complete terror, the dragon grew six more heads with gold crowns and a total of ten horns which filled me with immense fear and utter dread.
Pacing and becoming bigger with each and every step,
The beast shook itself in rage and threatened the throne and they that sat upon it; it was such a hideous sight, I cried and then violently wept.
Then a great ringing voice came from the throne and said, "No."
The dragon postured threatening and appeared to want to advance on the throne; Michael stepped that way, and again the voice said, "No."
Michael turned back to me.
"Behold," he said, pointing in the direction behind me.
I slowly turned to see the figure of a woman dressed brilliantly and blinding in clothes as bright as the sun.
She appeared to be standing upon the very moon, and on her beautiful head was a wreath made of twelve stars; I wanted to cry out to her, to tell her to quickly run.
The woman was pregnant, and she turned and began to cry out in labour pains.
She grimaced as her body convulsed in contractions and away from her the brightness began to drain.
As she stood clutching her swollen massive belly as if about to give birth,
The distracted dragon jumped from his place before the throne and pounced before the woman, his great tail swept a third of the stars from the thundering heavens and they fell to the earth.
She gave birth to a male child who was caught up to God.

The raging dragon watched as the child was taken to the throne, and when he turned back to the woman, he found that she had already fled; he rose up to chase her, and Michael the archangel said, "Behold."
I turned to watch him use both of his mighty and strong hands to pull a golden giant sword from its sheath and swing it high over his beautiful glowing head.
A Heavenly host of great warrior angels fell in behind him as the dragon's angels mustered behind him, waiting impatiently to be led.
Suddenly, against the dragon, Michael led the charge.
The Heavens filled with tremendous thunder and my body became paralyzed by an immense and powerful electrical charge…

The apostle John describes Daniel's ten kings as "horns" on the seven heads of a "beast." King Nebuchadnezzar saw the future governments of man as a beautiful image, but God saw them as beasts. Man sees government as beautiful and impressive and worships it, while God sees the governments of the world as beasts.

The seven heads John describes in the Book of Revelation I believe probably refer to the seven stages of the Roman Empire, the epitome of evil government. The seven kings, of whom "five have fallen, one is, and the other has not yet come." I believe the five "fallen" kings were the five Roman emperors before John's time; the sixth was Domitian, the emperor at the time John wrote; and the seventh will be the Antichrist, himself.

The Beast with Two Horns:

This figure is known as the false prophet. That he has two horns like a lamb, I believe may suggest that he will try to appear as gentle as the Lamb of God, but is very deceiving. He speaks like a dragon, eager to declare the very words of Satan. He will have the power to do great signs while in the presence of his master, the Antichrist. In this way will he deceive many into worshipping and following the Beast.

Chasms And Bridges Within The Heart

The Mark

Therefore rejoice, ye heavens, and ye that dwell in them. Woe to the inhabiters of the earth and of the sea! For the devil is come down unto you, having great wrath, because he knoweth that he hath but a short time.
(Revelation 12:12)

And I beheld another beast coming up out of the earth; and he had two horns like a lamb, and he spake as a dragon.
And he exerciseth all the power of the first beast before him, and causeth the earth and them which dwell therein to worship the first beast, whose deadly wound was healed.
And he doeth great wonders, so that he maketh fire come down from Heaven on the earth in the sight of men,
And deceiveth them that dwell on the earth by means of those miracles which he had power to do in the sight of the beast; saying to them that dwell on the earth, that they should make an image to the beast, which had the wound by a sword, and did live.
And he had power to give life unto the image of the beast, that the image of the beast should both speak, and cause that as many as would not worship the image of the beast should be killed.
And he causeth all, both small and great, rich and poor, free and bond, to receive a mark in their right hand or in their foreheads: and that no man might buy or sell, save he that had the mark, or the name of the beast, or the number of his name.
Here is wisdom. Let him that hath understanding count the number of the beast: for it is the number of a man; and his number is Six hundred threescore and six.
(Revelation 13: 13-18)

Amanda Perry

The times are changing.
Everything within this world is quickly and appointedly rearranging.
We are fastly approaching a time in this world,
Where the leader will promise and preach peace, while at the same time he will be wielding a sword.
This leader is both anti-Christian and Antichrist himself,
And the Bible says the resurrected Antichrist is literally indwelt by Satan himself.
A promoter of Antichrist will have an image of the Antichrist erected and will force one and all to worship it or face their own peril, is known as the Antichrist's false prophet.
As the Bible predicts, he has power to give utterance to the image and to call down fire from Heaven to destroy those who refuse to worship it and instead scoff at it.
It won't be long before everyone will be forced to bow the knee to the Antichrist or his image.
To bear his name or number on their forehead or right hand, or face the consequences and witness his evil and severe damage.
Consequences?
What are the consequences?
Those of us without what the Bible calls the mark of the beast will not be allowed to legally buy or sell.
If we publicly refuse to accept the mark of the beast, we will be tortured, beheaded, and forced to suffer in jail.
No one can receive the mark of the beast by accident.
It is a once-and-for-all decision that will forever condemn you to eternity without God; my friends, I'm telling you, the mark of the beast is permanent.
While many will be called to live in secret, to support one another through private markets,

Chasms And Bridges Within The Heart

Some will find themselves caught, singled out, dragged into public beheadings and different forms of tortures; living in a severe period of endless darkness.
This period will be the bloodiest season in the history of the world.
Those who take the mark of the beast will suffer affliction at the hand of God; will suffer the piercing of His mighty sword.
Those who refuse it will be martyred for His blessed cause.
Never has the choice been so stark, so plain, please make a choice before this time of darkness upon us falls.
God Himself gave name to this darkened period:

For then shall be great tribulation, such as was not since the beginning of the world to this time, no, nor ever shall be.
And except those days should be shortened, there should no flesh be saved: but for the elects sake those days shall be shortened.
(Matthew 24:21-22)

In all God's dealings with mankind, this is the shortest period He devised.
Yet, more Scripture is devoted to it than any other period except the life of Christ.
Despite that, this is clearly the most awful time in history.
It is also a merciful act of God to give as many souls as possible an opportunity to put their faith in Christ consistently.
We are to be the army of God with a massive job to do in a short time.
I pray that we may do it with willingness and eagerness and the courage that comes only from Him, a power most divine.
There are and will be countless lost souls in need of saving,
And we have the truth within us radiating.
When His wrath is also intensifying, it may be difficult to recognize the mercy of God.
Woe to those who believe the lie that God is only "love."
He is love, yes,

Amanda Perry

And His gift of Jesus as the sacrifice for our sin is the greatest evidence of this.
He is righteous and a God of justice and glory,
And it is not in His nature to allow sin to go unpunished or unpaid for, unfortunately.
We are engaged in a great worldwide battle with Satan himself for the souls of men and women,
But I have placed my faith and trust in the God who sits high whom there is none like Him.
Next is coming the ceremonial desecration of the temple in Jerusalem by the Antichrist.
This desecration shall include blasphemy against God, derogatory statements about God and Messiah, a denial of Christ's resurrection, and extreme profanity.
The Antichrist will also break his covenant with Israel and withdraw his promised guarantee of her safety.
Besides reviling all the Jews,
He will terrorize and slaughter believers in Jesus; believe me, in our future, extreme danger ensues…

I ask God now to bless you all in the perfect name of Jesus. May He always bless you and forever keep you and make His brilliant face to shine upon you, and give you eternal peace,
Amen

Chasms And Bridges Within The Heart

Come To Me

Come to Me...
Come to Me...
When you have no one to turn to
And no light through the darkness to guide you,
Take a deep breath and in the silence listen.
To talk to Me, you need no permission
Come to Me...
Come to Me...
When your journey turns dark and stormy,
Through it all, by your side I will be.
If it seems like no one around you understands,
Know that I will be there holding your hand.
Come to Me...
Come to Me...
When you feel like this world leaving,
Remember your faith and keep on believing.
You are strong enough to make it through.
I will always be right there to comfort and love you.
Come to Me...
Come to Me...

Amanda Perry

When the night is lonely and full of pain
And you feel like you are drowning in shame,
Just close your tear-filled eyes.
Remember that there is healing within the skies.
Come to Me…
Come to Me…
When it seems that all hope is forever lost,
There is a healing gift that comes without a cost.
Salvation for you is entirely free.
Open your heart and soon you will see.
Come to Me…
Come to Me…
My friend, know that I love you.
No other Love will you ever find as strong and true.
For you I was mocked and hated.
With My Blood you have been saturated.
Beaten, bruised, and crucified,
For you I gave my life; for you I freely died.
Come to Me…
Come to Me…

Chasms And Bridges Within The Heart

The American Spirit

I pledge Allegiance…
To the Flag…
Of the United States of America…
And to the Republic…
For which it stands…
One Nation…
Under God…

She proudly stands alone, both majestic and true;
The most beautiful picture of endless solitude.
The ageless soul of a woman encased in red, white, and blue
With stars and stripes that to the weary soul peace and strength they do renew.
Alone she's faced the storms of life;
The wicked wind and pelting rain, moth-ridden disease and ceaseless strife.
Others gave up, but no, not she,
And there she stands steadfast and firm for all the world to see.
She's had her share of troubles and woes,
But she always made it through, and still upon the wind's whispers she proudly blows.

Amanda Perry

Like her, America too knows growing grief and disturbing pain.
We've faced the raging wind; we've felt the stinging rain.
Just like her too, America and I still stand tall,
Though enemies and war may wear us down and beat us, I can honestly assure you that we will not fall.
Enemies may throw punches and kicks, we may take a horrible and significant blow,
But in the end we too just like the wind shall freely flow.
Each storm we weather only increases our wisdom and strength,
And abiding beneath and above this wondrous Nation, our God is the Leader to always and forever thank.
America and the American Flag, we know just what it is that we have to do.
We count on God our Father and our very dedicated and hard-working troops, and God willing, we always make it through.

Chasms And Bridges Within The Heart

My Dear Serenity

Always be fabulous and classy,
Be super silly and fun.
Go ahead and get dirty,
Dance brilliantly in the sun.
Be confident and proud,
Always be hungry for knowledge.
Follow your dreams and PLEASE
Do go to college.
Have lots of friends,
Be a woman of strength
And a child of God,
Be goofy and different;
It's okay to be a bit odd.
Always be yourself,
No matter what others may say.
Stay little as long as you can.
Never ever forget how to play.
Learn to change a tire
And the oil in your car.
Never ever depend on any man.
Find out exactly who you are.

Amanda Perry

Travel the world.
Have a love full of passion.
Marry a man with a heart;
Believe me, looks can and will fade like fashion.
Be a true friend,
Always stay true to your word,
Don't give into gossip;
You do not have to repeat what you heard.
Don't burn bridges.
It's right to admit when you're wrong.
Forgive and forget,
Play your favourite song,
Sing as loud as you possibly can,
Laugh until it truly hurts,
Fake it until you make it,
Find whatever works.
Wherever you go, never forget your way home,
Think of mommy always,
Pick up the phone…

I love you, baby girl, more than anything!
I am and always will be proud of you,
Mommy

Chasms And Bridges Within The Heart

The Creation, The Curse, And The Promise

Since eternity past, God the Father, Son, and Holy Ghost lived in unity and beautiful fellowship.
Then the Trinity decided to make a wondrous universe with an earth for life to forever dwell.
Creating an awesome array of creatures was the easy part- the risk developed on the last made.
For unlike other creatures, man and woman were made in God's own image with a Spirit.
That Spirit communicated with God, and everlasting harmony reigned as Earth was well cared for and protected.
The Freedom to do was great- limited by but one tree that the two humans were never to eat from.
At that forbidden tree, Satan disguised himself as an innocent and deceptive snake and asked the woman some serious questions.
"Did God really say they shouldn't eat from the tree?"
"Well, that's to keep you from becoming all knowing, powerful, and wise just like Him."
"Look at its fruit. It is beautiful and with just one bite you will know exactly what God knows and will be Jehovah's equal."

Amanda Perry

Eve was very confused, for this did not sound like what Adam had told her, but wouldn't it be so grand?!
"If God is so good, why would He keep this secret from us of being able to be just like Him- is He jealous?"
The firm, ripe, and juicy fruit was indeed delicious, and she quickly convinced Adam to taste, which very soon he did.
A small act? Every war, hatred, lie, murder, rape, and abuse came from this very moment.
The beauty of God's perfect Creation was now tainted with sin that affected every part with hideous death and decay.
God graciously provided Adam and Eve animal skins, for no more would they abide in Eden's perfect climate.
From now on there would be sweat for the food they ate and immensely great pain during childbirth.
Even their very own firstborn would murder their second born, starting the cycle of revenge and killing that has remained ongoing.
Yet God also made a promise that one would come who would crush Satan's head while being bruised.
"In the beginning was the Word, and the Word was with God, and the Word was God," clues us in to who.
For God's only Son Himself would come to teach, heal, and willingly offer His life on a Cross to destroy our Hellish death curse.
Our sins He would bear and in rising He would seal the Promise of eternal life.
For Jesus the cost was unbelievably high, and for us the reward is incredibly great- if we but accept.

Chasms And Bridges Within The Heart

Accept that I am a sinner, I've done wrong and severely need God's forgiveness to live with His eternal perfection.
Accept that Jesus Christ can do what I absolutely cannot- change my heart, make my dying Spirit alive to forever live with God.
This being God, the Promise of Heaven and a new Earth is sure, though pain lies in between- Choose now.
For God and all of His majestic creation cry out- this is what life is meant for- to know and love one's true Maker.
As humans, we either live eternally with or apart from God, and His great desire is that we choose which one.
Just as an earthly father cannot force love, neither does our Heavenly Father- He patiently waits.
Though He made all and knows beginning from end,
He waits and yearns that we believe and receive His great Love.
Then love and be loved by Jesus in life's hardships and delights, sharing that most amazing love with other lost children.
To work always in harmony with the One who made us
Makes life new again as our spirit is filled with brand-new life.
There will be dry days when we won't feel His Holy presence, but other days so full of It that we will want to shout for joy.
The terrific fact is that Our Father God, our Savior Jesus Christ, the Holy Spirit, is always with us and will never ever leave nor forsake us,
Amen.

Amanda Perry

Creation In The Garden Of Eden

When the Lord God made the heavens and the earth,
There were no plants or grain growing on the earth.
For the Lord God had not sent any rain,
And no one was there to cultivate the soil.
Water, a mist, came up out of the ground and watered all the land,
And the Lord God formed a man's body from the dust of the ground
and breathed into it the breath of life,
And the man became a living person.
Then the Lord God planted a garden in Eden, in the east, and there He
placed the man He had created…
A garden of vast and impressive beauty,
To stand and walk through this garden is a blessing from God; not at all
a mere duty.

A light glittering mist swirls all around me.
My skin feels tingly and refreshed, rejuvenated, as clean as it can ever
possibly be.
Dazzling drops of dew sparkle like diamonds upon the grass and
leaves.
Sunlight filters through the drops, creating millions of glittering prisms
that to the eyes do please.

Chasms And Bridges Within The Heart

The sky is an endless brilliant masterpiece painted with vibrant shades of the promising rainbow.
Like clouds, the colors gently shimmer across the vast openness of sky when the wind does begin to blow.
My senses come alive as I inhale the fragrant winds.
My soul is coming alive with the ecstasy it does send.
I close my eyes and slowly identify the scents of freshly-blooming roses, luscious scents of lavender, and vibrant scents of vanilla and honey.
Intoxicating exotic scents overtake my thoughts, and I gaze up at the sky which is breathtaking and sunny.
It is as if I have opened my eyes for the very first time.
Everything seems to sparkle and glitter; everything to my eyes is dazzling and sublime.
The tall flourishing grasses shimmer different shades of green as the breeze gently blows,
Twinkling trickles of crisp, refreshing, and cool water appear throughout this land and with it engulfing healing does flow.
The fragrant plants are wondrous to behold.
Thriving and flourishing, they grow as tall as I and produce massive blooms with every color being vibrant and bold.
My ears awaken to every sound, and my soul is filled with radiating peace.
The trickling water, the rustling of grass and leaves, the whispering wind: amazing comfort and relaxation they all release.
Suddenly up ahead in a clearing,
A funnel of swirling sand and dust slowly began appearing.

Around and around it quickly swirled, gaining immense speed,
A sound of rushing wind enveloped me; like someone from the Heavens had just breathed.
Immediately the swirling funnel stopped and disappeared.
I gasped as before me, lying on the ground and chest heaving with each breath, a real and alive man appeared.
The man was radiant and significantly gorgeous.
His skin appeared to shimmer and I was taken by surprise at its allureness.
He studied his arms and legs, fingers and toes, hands and feet,
A velvet smooth and musical tone erupted as a laugh from within his throat was both beautiful and sweet.
Eyes that glittered and danced as blue as the sky,
He inhaled a deep breath and, smiling gratefully, he did sigh.
His hair was brown and highlighted with rich gold,
The color to his eyes by it was made most bold.
Out of the depths of the garden came a voluminous and gentle voice:
"My son, Adam, this garden is yours to tend and to care for; it is for you to keep."
"You may eat from any fruit in the garden except fruit from one tree, from the Tree of the Knowledge of Good and Evil you will surely die if from it you shall eat."
Adam gazed around as if searching for this tree.
I quietly followed him through the garden to its center and a most beautiful and spectacular tree did we see.
Its trunk was massive and around it grew radiant blooming vines.
It grew immensely up in height as if a staircase to Heaven and to a God most divine.

Chasms And Bridges Within The Heart

Great swooping branches twisted and turned.
A most memorable sight into my mind it seemed to dominate and to burn.
Its branches were full of flowing thick leaves which were the colors of sunsets and glittered in the breeze.
I silently fell to my knees and praises and prayers my overflowing soul did release.
Never such beauty has the world ever seen;
Nothing can ever compare, not even in beautiful dreams.
The fruit of this tree was large in size.
A fragrance so sweet enveloped around it and taunting on the breezes it did fly.
Bright orange, yellow, and red,
All over this masterpiece of a tree this wondrous fruit did spread.
In the sunlight, the fruit appeared to glitter and glisten like sparkling jewels.
It would in no way be simple to follow and obey God's only rule.
Adam stood very silent and very still.
He was frozen in a trance, being held by God's own will.
The magnificent tree was reflecting back through his eyes.
His voice became a soft whisper: "If you shall eat from this Tree of the Knowledge of Good and Evil, you shall surely die."
Suddenly, he shook his head and slowly walked away.
I followed silently behind, alone near that beautiful tree was I afraid to stay.
The wind swirled around us again.
"It is not good for the man to be alone. I will make a companion who will help him."

Amanda Perry

In the clearing giant swelling funnels reappeared,
And running and flying out of them every kind of animal and bird suddenly appeared.
Forming a straight line, every animal waited before Adam to be named.
Adam thoughtfully and carefully chose a name for each and every one.
Amazingly they all bowed before him as if already completely tame.
Yet, for Adam, there was no companion of his own kind.
I watched as he blissfully fell into a very deep sleep; and I wondered what sort of dreams ran through his brilliant mind.
I watched in awe and fascination as Adam's skin on his torso opened and revealed sparkling white bones.
A glittering mist shaped like a man gently removed one of Adam's ribs and healed the open cut, and from Adam never came the sound of any moans.
The man of mist, whom I realized to be God, placed the rib in the dirt of the earth,
And from it a woman He did unearth.
She was beautiful and appeared angelic.
She was of a glistening pale peach color and her movements were most graceful and delicate.
Long and waving vibrant brown hair cascaded down her back and to her hips.
A permanent blush the color of the pink rose stained her perfect lips.
Brilliant prisms of dancing light were the blue windows to her glorious soul.
Velvet soft and black were the eyelashes that rimmed around her eyes.
Slowly, Adam rises up from where he had lied.

Chasms And Bridges Within The Heart

"At last!" He exclaimed and joy all around him and in him flowing began.
"She is part of my own flesh and bone! She will be called 'woman,' because she was taken out of a man…"
Now the serpent was the shrewdest of all the creatures the Lord God had made.
He waited patiently for Adam and the woman to pass by the Tree of the Knowledge of Good and Evil where he had made his home and silently stayed.
The woman was the first one to pass by the glorious tree.
He coiled around a branch and hissed most deceitfully:
"Really? Did God really say you must not eat any of the fruit in the garden?"
The woman gazed at the coiling length of the serpent and raised her beautifully arched eyebrows at the creature she was regarding.
"Of course we may eat it. It's only the fruit from this tree that we are not allowed to eat."
"God says we will die if we touch it and from it eat."
The serpent hissed violently and spoke words that were very believable:
"You will not die! God knows that your eyes will be opened when you eat it; you will become just like God, knowing everything, both good and evil."
The woman quickly became convinced,
So she ate some of the fruit and shared also with Adam and, at that moment, their eyes were fully opened and at their nakedness the two quickly winced.
The woman hurriedly tried to cover herself as warm tears fell from her eyes.
Adam quickly thought of tying together giant fig leaves for their nakedness to hide.

Amanda Perry

The rest of the day, Adam stood by the woman's side,
Tried to comfort her, but when they heard the Lord God walking
through the garden, they sheltered themselves among the trees to hide.
The swirling mists outlining a man's form came into sight.
A picture radiating with divine beauty, I inhaled a deep breath and held it within very tight.
A breathtaking warm yellow glow pulsates all around the gentle mists.
The serpent recoiled with a sudden and hate-filled hiss.
The mists shimmered and glittered as if made up of millions of tiny diamonds and sparkling jewels.
Radiant moonlight dazzled around Him embracing Him in pale glowing pools.
The magnificent garden paled in comparison to the splendor of God's swirling mists.
The most beautiful voice broke through the stillness of the night; a warm and comforting feeling enveloped me as if from the sun receiving a kiss.
"Where are you?"
Adam closed his eyes and slowly replied:
"I heard You coming, so I hid. I was afraid because I was naked, too."
"Who told you that you were naked?" The Lord God questioned.
"Have you eaten the fruit I commanded you not to eat?" God silently waited for a confession.
"Yes," Adam admitted, "but it was the woman you gave me who brought me the fruit, and I ate it."
Then the Lord God asked the woman, "How could you do such a thing? What to this decision made you commit?"
"The serpent tricked me," she quietly replied.
"That's why I ate it," she dejectedly sighed.

Chasms And Bridges Within The Heart

So the Lord God said to the hissing serpent:
"Because you have done this, you are singled out from all the domestic and wild animals of the whole earth to be cursed,"
"You will grovel in the dust as long as you live, crawling along on your belly never to resurf."
"From now on, you and the woman will be enemies, and your offspring and her offspring will be enemies."
"He will crush your head, and you will strike his heel."
Then He said to the woman:
"You will bear children with intense suffering and pain."
"And though your desire will be for your husband, he will be your master. Do not serve him in vain."
And to Adam He said:
"Because you listened to your wife and ate the fruit I told you not to eat, I have placed a curse on the ground."
"All your life you will struggle to scratch a living from it and it will grow thorns and thistles for you, though you will eat of its grains that will be found."
"All your life you will sweat to produce food until your dying day."
"Then you will return to the ground from which you came, for you were made from dust, and to the dust you will return always."
Then Adam named his wife Eve,
Because she would be the mother of all people everywhere, starting with their own children they would soon conceive.
Clothing made from animal skins
The Lord God made for each of them.

Amanda Perry

Then the Lord God said:
"The people have become as we are, knowing everything, both good and evil; what if they eat the fruit of the Tree of Life?"
He lovingly gazed at Adam and his wife.
So He banished Adam and his wife from the wondrous Garden of Eden, and He sent Adam out to cultivate the ground from which he had been made.
The Lord God then stationed mighty angelic beings and a flaming sword that flashed back and forth, forever guarding the way to the Tree of Life, and entry into Eden the angelic beings forever forbade.

Chasms And Bridges Within The Heart

Kenneth

A young life that had just begun,
Perseverance and passion in the veins did rapidly run.
Hopes and dreams were within his reaching grasp.
In the radiance of life he did bask.
A kind heart and innocently pure soul,
An aura all about him that made his beautiful being glow.
A beautiful and breathtaking smile
Could win the heart of any person most vile.
Bright eyes full of life, compassion, and love.
His mind and body was full of strength, and yet he was always as gentle as a dove.
Of others he was always accepting and caring.
He never had much but, what he did have, he was always willingly sharing.
In possession of a hilarious sense of humor,
A part of my life I wish he could have been sooner.
Always putting other people first,
His passion was life, it was his unquenchable thirst.
A very extraordinary and remarkable young man
Who unexpectedly left this life and gained entrance into the Promised Land…

Amanda Perry

It happened on a bitterly cold, snow-filled February day.
This young man, who had blessed my life with his presence, had been suddenly from this earth ripped away.
Why?
Why so soon?
These are unanswered questions that still in the back of my mind loom.
I'm sure that on that cold day while he was lying in the snow
That he was surrounded by Heaven's glorious Angels and their warm radiating glow.
Their voices soft and velvet began singing him a wondrous song of miraculous healing,
Diminishing the bitter cold and all of the intense pain that he was feeling.
A most enveloping and glorious light shines bright before his eyes.
A feeling of longing and welcoming washes over him as his last breath he happily sighs.
A Man wearing glorious robes of white
Walks through the light, wearing a smile of welcoming delight.
To the young man He gently goes.
Gathering the young man up into His arms, His warmth from His beautiful body passionately flows.
The young man's cold and colorless face slowly begins to develop a most radiant blush.
A Holy transformation begins as all throughout his broken body, pulsating ribbons of healing quickly begin to rush.
Sweet and tender butterfly kisses fall upon the young man's snow-covered eye lashes.
Like a butterfly's glittering wings, his eyelids begin to flutter as from the Man in white new life quickly passes.

Chasms And Bridges Within The Heart

A hand filled with tremendous love and healing
Is gently placed on the young man's chest, and very faintly He feels the beating.
Intoxicating fragrances of things sweet but unknown
Swirl into his senses and, taking his first breath, he quietly moans.
He can hear sounds of nature that to him never sounded so sweet.
A voice most beautiful and compassionate:
"My sweet Kenneth, arise," and suddenly, his eyes open for the owner of the voice he knew he just had to meet…

Dedicated to Kenneth Ray Cremeans

He was an amazing young man and an even better brother. He was beautiful, through and through. For reasons unknown to us, God decided to call him home to Heaven. Maybe, he had suffered enough here on earth already. Maybe, he wasn't meant to see how bad this world would become, or maybe, Heaven needed a most beautiful and one-of-a-kind brightly shining angel. Whatever the reason, I know that he is happier and healthier, and right where he wants to be. He's my own family's guardian angel and watches over us every day. He is missed terribly and thought of every day. May you rest in peace for always, Kenneth. I know that you are one of the brightest shining angels in Heaven! We love you, and can't wait for that moment when we can be together again.

Love you always and forever.

Amanda Perry

For You My God

Inside of this body, emotions are raging.
Inside of this temple, the spirit is blazing.
Inside of this chest, the heart is pulsating.
Inside of this throat, the voice is praising…

For You, My God
Alone are worthy
For You, My God
Was blind but now I see
For You, My God
A song of endless praise
For You, My God
A follower until my last of days

Outside of this body, eyes are joyfully crying.
Outside of this body, lips are beautifully smiling.
Outside of this body, hands are raising.
Outside of this body, knees bow down and are praising.

Chasms And Bridges Within The Heart

For You, My God
Alone are worthy
For You, My God
Was blind but now I see
For You, My God
A song of endless praise
For You, My God
A follower until my last of days

Throughout this body, Your Spirit is flowing.
Throughout this body, Your Light is glowing.
Throughout this body, Your Blood is cleansing.
Throughout this body, Your Healing is rinsing…

For You, My God
Alone are worthy
For You, My God
Was blind but now I see
For You, My God
A song of endless praise
For You, My God
A follower until my last of days

Upon this body Your Mark is seeping
Upon this body Your Seal will forever be keeping
Upon this body Your Grace is saving
Upon this body Your Love will forever be remaining

Amanda Perry

For You, My God
Alone are worthy
For You, My God
Was blind but now I see
For You, My God
A song of endless praise
For You, My God
A follower until my last of days

Blessing this body with Your wisdom and knowledge.
Blessing this body with a foundation that's firm and solid.
Blessing this body with Your talents and gifts to use.
Blessing this body for the choice it chose to choose.

For You, My God
Alone are worthy
For You, My God
Was blind but now I see
For You, My God
A song of endless praise
For You, My God
A follower until my last of days
For You, My God

Chasms And Bridges Within The Heart

The Triumphal Entry

It was the time of the Passover, and the city of Jerusalem was thriving. Hundreds upon hundreds of men, women, and children from all over were here to beautiful Jerusalem arriving.
Under the bluest of skies, the people joyously traversed.
Little children ran up ahead, while their parents along with others about Jesus and His miracles and preaching did converse.
He had not come to Jerusalem for the Passover the previous year. Instead, He had spent the week with His disciples in the warm vastness of the desert after feeding a large multitude on five barley loaves and two fish; more than just a man, to many He was the long-awaited Messiah, the true Son of God He did appear.
Everyone walking was busily talking about Jesus, and all were hoping "the Nazarene" would come to Jerusalem this year so they could see Him.
Their excitement was contagious, for it was like a cup overflowing with wine, easily flowing up and over the cup's brim.
The sound of flutes and drums soon became acquainted with dozens of beautiful singing voices.
Even the wilderness around them seemed to come alive and along with them did rejoice.

Amanda Perry

Men, women, and children singing, laughing, and merrily dancing,
Even the donkeys and other animals seemed to be happily prancing.
Most of the people could only talk of the many wonders that Jesus did perform,
Retaining nothing of the lessons He did to them willingly inform.
They were eager to see Jesus perform miracles, greedy to eat bread that cost them nothing, hopeful to see their enemies crushed, humiliated, and even killed.
He hadn't been born to do what men wanted, but what God willed.
How would Jesus do it? Some people began to question.
How would God's Son bring redemption to these people who only wanted to be entertained? They could find no suggestions.
If Jesus did not do what they wanted or expected,
They would turn on Him; He would be terribly rejected.
As the people reached the gates of Jerusalem, some caught a glimpse of His mother, Mary, standing alongside His brethren.
Before the company could go any further, they heard other people gallantly shouting: "Praise God for the Son of David! Bless the one who comes in the Name of the Lord! Praise God in the highest Heaven!"
The swell of voices grew until it was most deafening.
These people were welcoming Jesus into the city of Jerusalem, what an amazing and awesome blessing!
Riding upon the back of a donkey was the Son of God.
A great and wondrous multitude of people spread their garments down in front of where the donkey trod.
Jesus was a picture of divine and glorious beauty.
To welcome Him into the city and proclaim Him the Messiah was a gift from God, not at all a duty.

Chasms And Bridges Within The Heart

His face was beautiful and appeared to be glowing.
A current of acceptance and unconditional love from Him seemed to be continually flowing.
The people walking along with Him began to joyously sing:
"Hosanna to the Son of David: Blessed is He that cometh in the Name of the Lord; Hosanna in the highest," their voices with praise and worship did ring.
More people began stripping branches from trees and spreading them over the road.
Others held theirs and fanned them as riding past them Jesus did go.
At the people He smiled and waved,
A lightness of heart within them He easily made.
Eyes that sparkled and brilliantly danced,
People felt loved and wanted right at the first glance.
As He passed the children, He laughed with glee.
He loved every child with undying passion, this almost everyone could see.
The babies that the mother's held, to them He gave a precious kiss.
Not one of the babies cried, it seemed they too were enveloped in a peaceful and celebrating bliss.
As He rode through the gates,
The people were not aware that He soon would hold the keys to their eternal fate...

Amanda Perry

The Den Of Thieves

It is written, My house shall be called the House of Prayer; but ye have made it a Den of Thieves. **(Matthew 21:13)**

The crowd of people continued to follow Jesus into the Temple complex, which was overflowing with even more people and lavishly-laden tables with all sorts of items to sell.
Spices, garments, wooden crates that housed doves and pigeons; people were buying and selling within the Temple, and Jesus's eyes beheld every last sinister detail.
He heard the voices of the merchants trying to find a buyer.
He heard the tinkling of money as it exchanged greedy hands to feed a most loathsome desire.
The sound of people bartering reached His innocent ears.
Lambs and goats were fenced up and bleating, doves and pigeons were cooing for freedom; as He looked around, His beautiful blue eyes filled with sparkling tears.
Suddenly, up towards Heaven, Jesus raised his hand.
At the sound of His voice, every man's attention He did demand:
"Jerusalem, the faithful city, she that was full of justice, has become a harlot!"

Chasms And Bridges Within The Heart

To Jesus, the people with their greed and want, had turned the Temple away from God and had painted with their sins the Holy walls scarlet.
People began screaming as Jesus broke the jars containing money.
The priests began shouting angrily as they along with the merchants started running.
As the money scattered upon the ground,
Many people began greedily crawling to see how much of it could be counted and found.
Doves and pigeons flew out from among the Temple's columns and out across the city into the freedom of the vast blue sky.
Sheep and goats were bleating and running wild among the surprised crowd as Jesus began overturning the tables and, as He overturned each one, He began to freely and openly cry.
Jesus ran up the steps that led into the beautiful Temple and began shouting to the crowd,
"This, is a House of prayer! And you have turned it into a den of thieves!" His words were clear and loud.
He then turned and walked inside the Temple of God and raised His head toward Heaven.
His beautiful and pure lips silently moved as He stood there and to His Father prayed and thanked Him for His blessing.
His eyes were full of love and compassion.
He turned around, looking at the wondrous Temple, and then to the people He spoke in this fashion:
"The Temple is not mere stone. It is the House of God. It cannot be destroyed as long as God lives here."
He became suddenly quiet as His glittering eyes fell and rested upon a chief priest of the Temple that stood to Him very near.

Amanda Perry

"Destroy this Temple…"
"And in three days I will make it rise again…"
The high priest smiled and looked doubtfully at Him.
"It took centuries to build this Temple. Do you honestly think you could rebuild it within only three days?"
Jesus pulled His away from the high priest and upon the Heavens He fixed His gaze.
"You have indeed said it…"
"But you have not understood…"
The high priest drew in a deep breath and proudly stood.
"Rabbi, I understand better than you think I ever could."
The high priest then turned away from Jesus and slowly went inside. He believed that this Jesus was an extraordinary man and very aggravated, he sighed…
A great multitude of people sat and stood around Jesus in the Temple as His beautiful voice echoed and carried off the walls as He lovingly preached and taught.
Rapturous expressions were painted across each and every face. They finally saw and met Jesus, the one who for so long a time they all continually sought.
The Temple was basked in the radiating volumes of Jesus's sweet voice.
Every person there gazed into His beautiful and precious face; not one eye was dry, but every eye became adoringly moist.
He was their friend, brother, father, and king.
Every word He spoke was absolute truth and with His promises did ring.
Their shepherd, their guiding light, their Savior;
He had come to save the entire world. He had come to change the world's sinister and ugly behavior.

Chasms And Bridges Within The Heart

Not a sound other than His voice could be heard.
It was as if even the outside world, including all of nature, was hanging onto His every precious word.
A warm and welcoming glow seemed to fall around and upon Him.
Peace flowed from His body and reached out into the multitude and embraced each one of them.
"Blessed are the eyes that see what you see. For I tell you many kings and prophets have desired to see what you now see, and have not seen it. To hear what you now hear, and have not heard it."
His voice carried with it a loving comfort that to every person it did commit.
"I thank You, Father, for hiding these things from the learned and the wise and revealing them to the innocent and the simple. For He who would be the first must be your slave, just as the Son of Man came not to be served, but to serve and to give His life as a ransom for many."
Jesus raised His hands and still the multitude's attention He was commanding.
"Come to Me, all who labour and are heavy laden, and I will give you rest…"
"Come, O blessed of My Father, and inherit the Kingdom prepared for you from the very foundation of the world…"
"For I was hungry and you gave Me food…"
"I was thirsty and you gave Me drink…"
"I was a stranger and you welcomed Me…"
"I was naked and you clothed Me…"
"I was a prisoner and you visited Me…"
"I was sick and you came to Me…"

Amanda Perry

"You will surely ask: When did we do this for You?"
"Whoever does this to the least of my brethren, he does it unto Me…"
Jesus stood up and smiled for, at the entrance, a crowd of mothers had brought their babies and young ones for the Messiah to see.
He walked over to them, not aware of the priests standing nearby.
The babe's and children surrounded Him and not even one did cry.
He gently cradled a little one in His arms and laughed as the child exclaimed, "Son of David."
The priests listened and watched and became angry and very agitated.
"By what authority do You do these things?" They demanded.
"Before I answer, I will ask you a question," Jesus commanded.
"From where did John the Baptist receive authority to baptize… from Heaven or from men?"
The priests looked at one another and no answer to Jesus could they send.
"We don't… we don't know… we cannot tell!"
The priests were so angry that they had begun to yell.
"Very well, you tell Me nothing. Nor will I tell you by what authority I do these things."
Jesus started walking toward the doors of the Temple but turned back to the priests and loudly His voice did ring:
"John the Baptist came to you in righteousness, but you did not believe him. Even when you saw that there were sinners who believed and truly repented. They will get into the Kingdom of Heaven before you do."
Jesus turned and continued walking toward the doors, for His teaching was for now over; the evening was falling upon them, the day was finished and through…

Chasms And Bridges Within The Heart

Through This

Lord, our troubles
Are so great,
We don't know what to do;
The price for our iniquity
Is finally coming due.
The world is crumbling
All about;
No safe place can be found.
Right is wrong,
Wrong is right;
The change is quite profound.
Lord, we need
Your guiding light
To lead us out of here;
We'll focus on
Your Word and prayer
To take away our fear.

Amanda Perry

Temptations of
This dying world
We'll rule out and let go;
Give our burdens
All to You,
Shed all worldly woe.
That's how we'll
Get through this, Lord,
Fixed on Heaven above,
Assured of your
Protection, help,
And everlasting love.

Chasms And Bridges Within The Heart

Atonement

*They gave him vinegar to drink mingled with gall: and when he had tasted thereof, he would not drink.
And they crucified him, and parted his garments, casting lots: that it might be fulfilled which was spoken by the prophet, They parted my garments among them, and upon my vesture did they cast lots.
And sitting down they watched him there;
And set up over his head his accusation written, This Is Jesus The King of The Jews.
Then we're there two thieves crucified with him, one on the right hand, and another on the left.
And they that passed by reviled him, wagging their heads,
And saying, Thou that destroyest the temple, and buildest it in three days, save thyself. If Thou be the Son of God, come down from the cross.
Likewise also the chief priests mocking him, with the scribes and elders, said,
He saved others: himself he cannot save. If he be the King of Israel, let him now come down from the cross, and we will believe him.
He trusted in God; let him deliver him now, if he will have him: for He said, I am the Son of God.
The thieves also, which were crucified with him, cast the same in his teeth.*
(Matthew 27:34-44)

Amanda Perry

But he was wounded for our transgressions, he was bruised for our iniquities; the chastisement of our peace was upon Him; and with his stripes we are healed. **(Isaiah 53:5)**

"…I Am…"
"…And you will see the Son of Man seated at the right hand of power…"
"…And coming on the clouds of Heaven."
All eyes were upon Caiaphas, the high priest,
The whispering and quiet laughter among those who were assembled suddenly ceased.
Silence…
Silence…
Caiaphas glared at the Man standing before him and, suddenly, he screamed as he tore his clothes with sudden and fierce violence.
"Blasphemy!" Caiaphas screamed.
"You heard Him! He speaks blasphemy!" The hatred in his eyes brightly gleamed.
"We need no witnesses, his verdict… His verdict shall be death."
The assembled came forward and violently spit in His face and whispered obscene words to Him under their breath.
Laughter…
Laughter as they slapped His beautiful face, laughter as they struck His perfect body with their walking sticks, and laughter as after every assault they mockingly called Him 'Master.'
Surrendered into the hands of soldiers, He was beaten with chains, with merciless fists, and kicked down to the ground.
He did not fight back, He did not cry, nor did He ever make a sound.

Chasms And Bridges Within The Heart

One of His disciples, called Peter, stood among the cheering crowd.
Tears fell freely from his eyes as Jesus was beaten and mocked; when his Master's eyes fell upon him, he groaned aloud.
He made his way toward the entrance.
A man grabbed him and violently shook him as he spoke,
"Haven't I seen you in the company of the Galilean… yes, you are one of his faithful disciples!"
"Quiet, please, I've never even met the Man… I… I… I don't know Him," Peter shuddered as he answered upon the man's insistence.
He gazed at Jesus and gasped for breath as his tear-filled eyes traced the drops of blood cascading down His face.
Another man pointed at him and exclaimed, "I know you, you are Peter… a disciple of Jesus…" the people around him began calling out his name as sweat poured down his face and his blood and heart did begin to race.
"I do not know the man!"
Peter fell to the ground as he watched a chain violently smite Jesus's cheek.
He closed his eyes, believing he would die if he took one more peak.
Weakly, he stood to his feet and stumbled to the doors.
A woman's intense stare into his eyes startlingly bores.
"I have seen you before… you are one of them."
"You're wrong… I swear to you that I do not know Him!"
Peter pointed to Jesus as he spoke,
Then, suddenly, he remembered His Master's words and began to violently choke:
"I say to you…"
"Before the cock crows…"
"Three times you will deny me…"
He ran out the doors and into the darkness and, as he ran, he kept screaming, "I am unworthy…. I am unworthy!"

Amanda Perry

"Release Him!"
Pleaded a man who was once a disciple, but was now tortured by his act of greedy sin.
His body trembled and was drenched with gleaming sweat.
Tears fell from his eyes as he pleaded with the priests, leaving his face stained and wet.
"Take back the silver…. take it… I have sinned; I have betrayed blood that is innocent!"
"Take back the silver… innocent don't want it," he said with great temperament.
"Judas, you delivered the criminal, so the silver is the gift to you that we bestow."
"Take the money… your money, Judas, and go!"
Judas held the pouch of silver in his hand.
His hand trembled violently at the high priest's last command.
He threw the pouch to the ground and screamed.
The priests watched as the silver fell out and in the firelight gleamed…
Judas was weak, and his body convulsed violently.
He covered his ears and banged his head upon the bricks as sinister voices began tormenting him silently.
Trickles of blood slowly ran down his face.
He laughed and giggled as inside his chest he felt his heart suddenly race.
He clawed viciously at his itching and burning skin.
His vision became blurred and then he saw them…
"Judas," They continuously chanted.
They were coming for him, children of the darkness, and they had only one wish that for Judas they granted.

Chasms And Bridges Within The Heart

He shuddered and screamed as he tied the rope around the tree branch
and around his neck the other end he quickly slung.
"Judas," the voices cried as he stepped off the rock and lifeless from the
tree he hung…
The next morning dawned a beautiful day,
But for many it appeared dark, and worrisome, and never once ceasing
to their God did they pray.
The sky was clear and a magnificent blue.
The end was drawing near, the prophecies once foretold were now
coming true.
Jesus was tied with ropes and bound with multiple heavy chains.
The chief priests and his assembled brought Him before Pilate, the
governor, like this, heavily detained.
"What accusations do you bring against this man?"
Caiaphas looked at the crowd and raised his hand.
"He has violated our Sabbath, Consul… He has seduced the people…
taught disgusting, hideous doctrines."
"Isn't He the prophet that you welcomed into Jerusalem a few days
ago?" Pilate asked concerned.
"He has become the leader of a forceful and violent sect… who
worship and hail Him as the Messiah… the King promised to the
Jews… paying tribute to the emperor He has forbidden to His
followers."
Pilate stared at Jesus and then motioned Him forward, promoting from
the crowd chanting and hollers.
Pilate watched Jesus closely as he asked his question:
"Are You the King of the Jews…"
Jesus lifted His eyes and stared directly into Pilate's.
"Yes, it is as you say," He answered without defiance.

Amanda Perry

It was the governor's custom to release one prisoner to the crowd each year during the Passover celebration-anyone that the people chose. They were currently holding a notorious murderer… Barabbas… Pilate thought that surely, the murderer, the people would choose to dispose.
"Which of the two men would you have me release to you?"
"The murderer, Barabbas… or Jesus, King of the Jews?"
The crowd erupted in screaming Barabbas's name.
Pilate took a step back, surprised and confused; surely these people played with him a game.
"Again I will ask you: Which of these two men should I release to you?"
"Free Barabbas," the crowd's shouts continued.
"What would you have me do with Jesus the King of the Jews?"
The crowd pointed at Jesus and from their hate-filled mouths their answer violently spewed:
"Crucify Him!"
"Crucify Him!"
"Crucify Him!"
Jesus gazed out at the people, His heart having nothing but love for them.
Pilate shuddered as his insides tightened.
The crowd continued shouting as their hatred and lust for bloodshed heightened.
"I will chastise Him…but then I shall set Him free…"

Silence…
The crowd was filled with deafening silence…
They were thirsting for His pain, hungering for the acts of violence.
All eyes were on Him,
The Man that was tied to a post, and as the soldiers circled and mocked Him, the crowd began their chanting again.

Chasms And Bridges Within The Heart

Jesus lifted His eyes to Heaven and to His Father He prayed.
His faith remained strong and with Him His Father stayed.
The sound of tearing flesh as the soldiers take turns lashing Him with reeds.
The sight of trickling blood as His wounds open and bleed.
The sound of His chains as He's moved with each lash.
The laughter of the soldiers as they beat Him, spit upon Him, mock Him; they believe He is beneath them, appearing as nothing but trash.
Welts are forming upon His skin.
He falls to His knees and the priests smile and laugh, thinking that they're getting their revenge.
He slowly rises back upon His feet.
The soldiers chose a different form of violence, one with leather strips and nails on the end, to make Jesus admit defeat.
Jesus closed His eyes and prayed continuously.
His hair, wet with sweat and blood, hung about His face and shoulders loosely.
His hands trembled and shook as His body began going into shock.
The first blow from the soldier with this new weapon from His body His breath did knock.
The nails pierced deep within.
When jerked away, they pulled out chunks of His skin.
Gasping for breath,
The crowd stood in wonder and awe that He had not yet given in to death.
Trickles of blood became great running torrents.
The soldiers became angry and heightened their beating, thinking the reason that He didn't give up was their poor performance.
One right after another the lashes kept coming.
In His chest, Jesus's heart was fiercely drumming.

Amanda Perry

The soldiers laughed as His blood splattered upon their face.
Upon Jesus's body, covered with blood, welts, and open gashes, there was not left one little place.
His beautiful eyes became bloodshot and swollen.
His nose was pouring with blood, it had by a soldier's hand been broken.
Lips that brought truth into existence became misshapen and sliced open.
His body was badly bruised and in places broken…
Amidst the crowd that was joyfully celebrating stood a woman, steadfast and strong.
Her eyes never left Jesus, her Son, for she knew that this was the way God had commanded; this was where her Son did belong.
Her eyes welled up with compassionate and sorrowful tears
As before her eyes memories of her and her Son play like a movie, featuring all of their past years.
She holds her breath with every sound of tearing flesh.
This is her Son's destiny; this will indeed make the world blessed.
Her heart races as His blood is spilled upon the ground.
She moans as He suffers in silence, never making a sound.
She watches as skin is ripped from His body.
She feels weak and her legs become shaky and wobbly.
"My Son… When will You choose to be delivered of this?"
She questions and her voice is breaking.
Jesus looks into her eyes and immediately she's filled with comfort, knowing that the sins of the world, her Son, Jesus of Nazareth, is from this world taking.
Weeping…
Among the laughter and mocking there is also heard weeping.
Along with torrents of running blood, tears from the believer's eyes violently flow, streaming.

Chasms And Bridges Within The Heart

Lamentation…
Great and sorrowful lamentation.
The Son of God is dying for this perverted and wicked generation.
Praying…
She is finding her strength and the will to go on with her faith in God staying….

A pool of blood surrounds Jesus' feet and stains the white stones.
He falls to His knees and silently moans.
His body is heaving and severely convulsing.
His body is weak as His blood from His body is rushing and pulsing.
He places His battered head against the post, and the beating ceases.
They untie His bound hands, and He falls limply onto the blood-soaked ground and a guttural sigh He slowly releases.
The soldiers placed Jesus in the common hall.
There, His name, they mockingly did call.
They continued to spit in His disfigured face.
Each one of them violently punched His broken body, a part of skin not covered in bruises and blood there was not left a trace.
A crown of thorns they wove together and placed upon His beautiful head.
The thorns were pushed in deep and pierced His skin which violently gushed blood and continuously bled.
Upon His wounded body, they placed a scarlet robe.
And bowing down before Him, they sneered and mocked:
"Hail, King of the Jews! The greatest story ever told!"
Then, He was once again brought before Pilate,
And as the crowd gazed upon Him and demanded His Crucifixion,
He stood before them broken, bleeding, and silent.

Amanda Perry

Pilate called for a bowl of water and washed his hands.
"It is you who want to Crucify Him, not I... look you to it... I am innocent of His blood," he did demand...
The cross was placed before Him.
He knelt and, upon the coolness of the wood, He rested His cheek and chin.
With trembling hands, Jesus embraced His cross and silently prayed.
The soldiers pulled Him to His feet, and He gasped for air as the burden of His cross fell upon His shoulders.
The gazes from the crowd were gazes that burned with hatred and with revenge smoldered.
As He walked, soldiers behind Him slashed His back with a whip.
The crowd of people cheered with glee as Jesus stumbled and tripped.
People came forward and began throwing stones.
Jesus's vision blurred with the intense pain from broken and cracked bones.
Swirling in front of His blood-red eyes were people's smiling and laughing faces.
Sound was slowly fleeing from His ears, and a muffled ringing was taking its place.
His hands were trembling.
The lightness of day into darkness began receding.
A man appeared from out of the shadows and violently ran to shove Him.
Jesus stumbled and fell to the ground; the cross came slamming down upon Him.
The soldiers whipped slashes upon His head,
The ground around His body already covered with red.
The world around Him blurred and dizzyingly it spun.
"Behold, I make all things new," were His words that inside His ears rung.

Chasms And Bridges Within The Heart

He slowly stood to His feet and carried once more His cross upon His shoulders.
It was so heavy and large that, to Him, it was more like carrying boulders.
One of the soldiers struck Him forcefully on the back.
Jesus stumbled and dropped His cross as blood poured up into and out of His mouth, blood no longer red but black.
Jesus lay on the ground, His robes stained and matted with blood and dirt.
Even though His body was convulsing and shaking with shock, the soldiers continued whipping Him, making every wound throb and hurt.
Jesus could no longer hold the cross alone, so the soldiers commanded a man named Simon to help Him.
Simon lifted the cross and helped Jesus to His feet.
He gazed upon the face of Him and found that he could not speak.
Under all the blood, all the matted hair, under all the bruises Simon found and held Jesus' stare.
Tears formed in Simon's eyes as he saw endless love and compassion, forgiveness, peace, and hope within the eyes that absolutely no one ever will be able to compare.
Jesus could barely stand.
Simon willingly carried the cross while holding Jesus's one blood-stained and dirt-covered hand.
People among the crowd reached their hands up to Heaven,
Crying out to God and for His mercy pleading.
His mouth was dry and cracked with blood, His arms He could no longer feel or move, and His head was filling with dizzy darkness.
His heart He could barely feel beating as the whip cracked open His skin with sudden and intense sharpness.

"I am the good Shepherd... I lay down My life for my sheep... no one takes My life from me... but I lay it down of my own accord... I have power to lay it down... and power to take it up again... this power, it's from my Father."
Jesus heard His own voice ringing in His ears and knew that with Him still remained God the Father...

Golgotha, a place of a skull, was where Jesus was led.
He could not stand, nor could He walk. He had to crawl upon jagged rocks that turned red from His entire body that bled.
The soldiers kicked Him down upon His cross and violently tied His arms and legs to it.
As He lay there upon His cross. He stared at the sky which now had giant, billowing clouds moving across it very quick.
He turned His head to the left and gazed upon the priests.
He turned His head to the right and seeing His mother, Mary, a weakened breath He did release.
A nail was placed upon His right hand.
His body jerked as down upon it a hammer heavily slammed.
Blood flowed forth as if from a springing fountain of water.
Jesus moaned as the hammer slammed faster and harder.
His left hand violently began to shake as the nail pierced through His skin.
Mary cried out in agony as she watched her Son suffer in silence by the hands of men.
As the nail was pounced into His feet,
Tears made out of blood fell from His eyes:
"Father, forgive them..." Never was there another voice that sounded so sweet.

Chasms And Bridges Within The Heart

"Father…" He whispered as the hammer drove the nail deeper.
"My Father… My God…" His voice was fading; it was getting weaker.
"They do not know… Lord, they do not know…"
He whispered as the hammer forced the final blow.
The priests sneered as a sign was placed above His head.
'This is Jesus, The King of the Jews,' the sign read.
The cross was lifted up and set into place.
Sneering smiles spread across the priest's and soldiers' face.
"If You are the Son of God, why don't You save Yourself?"
Spoke the thief hanging on the cross to His right, wild and by evil mislead.
"Prove to us… You are who You say You are."
The blood pouring from the wounds in His hands and feet looked as black as tar.
The crowd cheered as Caiaphas, the high priest, began to speak,
"If He is the Messiah… I say, indeed, let Him come down from the cross… so that we may see and believe."
Jesus closed His eyes.
"Father, forgive them… they know not what they do…" Jesus shakily replies.
"Listen… He prays for you…" The thief on His left cries.
"We deserve this," he says to the thief on Jesus's right.
"But He… He… He does not… I have sinned… and my punishment is just… I ask only that You remember me, Lord… when You enter into Your kingdom," he said, crying openly in the people's sight.
Jesus gazed at the man and whispered:
"I tell you… on this day you shall be with Me… in Paradise."
The thief shuddered with thankfulness and praised Jesus for saving his life…

Amanda Perry

As the hours passed, the sky grew dark with ominous clouds.
At the bottom of the cross, Jesus's blood flows into pools and spreading it does surround.
Jesus lifts His head up to stare into the sky.
His body is filled with pain, and His mouth is severely dry.
His tears are now drops of blood, and His eyes are no longer blue but blood red.
Wind...
Wind begins to blow the matted hair upon His head.
Thunder...
Thunder breaks through the silence and puts people's thoughts all asunder.
Mary stands to her feet and very shakily she does stand.
The wind whips all around them, gaining enough force to lift rocks and sand.
The soldiers watch the rolling, ominous clouds as the day fades away.
The priests and elders begin leaving, in a storm they refuse to stay.

Jesus's body trembles, and He cries for a drink.
A soldier dips a sponge into vinegar and reaches it to Him, while away his own falling tears he rapidly does blink.
"My God..." Jesus cries as He looks toward Heaven.
"Why have You forsaken Me?"
Jesus looks back to the remains crowd.
His lips tremble as His words are spoken and amplified loud:
"It is accomplished... Father, into Your hands I commend My spirit..."
He looks again to the sky.
With one last breath, He is set free and to His Kingdom His soul does fly.
Rain...
Washing away all of the blood and pain.

Chasms And Bridges Within The Heart

Violent trembles shake the earth.
Tombs of once-godly men and women are suddenly opened and unearthed.
The Temple and its curtain split in two.
People ran screaming everywhere; they did not know what to do.
The soldiers feared Jesus still alive,
So one of them grabbed a spear and thrust it into His side.
Blood gushed forth, splattering all who were near.
Soldiers ran away driven entirely by fear.
Mary slowly walked up and gently caressed and kissed the feet of her Son.
Into the wind and rain, she whispered:
"It is done…"

Early on Sunday morning, as the new day was dawning, Mary Magdalene and the other Mary went out to see the tomb. Suddenly, there was a great earthquake, because an angel of the Lord came down from Heaven and rolled aside the stone and sat upon it. His face shone like lightning, and his clothes were as white as snow. The guards shook with fear when they saw him, and they fell into a dead faint.

Then the angel spoke to the women. "Do not be afraid!" He said. "I know you are looking for Jesus, who was crucified. He isn't here! He has been raised from the dead, just as He said would happen. Come, see where His body was lying. And now, go quickly and tell His disciples He has been raised from the dead, and He is going ahead of you into Galilee. You will see Him there. Remember, I have told you."

The women ran quickly from the tomb. They were very frightened but also filled with great joy, and they rushed to find the disciples to give them the angel's message. And as they went, Jesus met them. "Greetings!" He said. And they ran to Him, held His feet, and worshipped Him. Then, Jesus said to them, "Don't be afraid! Go tell my brothers to leave for Galilee, and they will see me there."

As the women were on their way into the city, some of the men who had been guarding the tomb went to the leading priests and told them what had happened. A meeting of all the religious leaders was called, and they decided to bribe the soldiers. They told the soldiers, "You must say, 'Jesus's disciples came during the night while we were sleeping, and they stole His body.' If the governor hears about it, we'll stand up for you and everything will be all right." So the guards accepted the bribe and said what they were told to say. Their story spread widely among the Jews, and they still tell it today.

Then the eleven disciples left for Galilee, going to the mountain where Jesus had told them to go. When they saw Him, they worshipped Him-but some of them still doubted!

Jesus came and told His disciples, "I have been given complete authority in Heaven and on earth. Therefore, go and make disciples of all the nations, baptizing them in the name of the Father and the Son and the Holy Spirit. Teach these new disciples to obey all the commands I have given you. And be sure of this: I am with you always, even to the end of the age."

Chasms And Bridges Within The Heart

Coming To A Theater Near You

I love to write about the past,
But the roles for the future have already been cast.
We each have been given a very special part to play.
Our lives have been anointed; we've each been selected for this very day.
This is the feature presentation that the whole world's been waiting for.
The Holy Spirit is our teacher, and Jesus Christ mans the door.
Our scripts aren't written on paper; they're written on our heart.
So if we don't know the author, we can't in any way play out our part.
The opening date hasn't yet been released, but I know it's coming very soon.
I've been asked to spread the Word; do you see the harvest moon?

Amanda Perry

The name of the feature is "The End of Time." It's the last to be played on earth.
Our Father has been preparing us for this since the day of our new birth.
As I said, we each play a part; there is no one immune.
This epic feature is about to unfold; Jesus is coming soon.
The Bible tells us exactly how this will end; this preview has been published for years.
But as in everything, it has its critics, they will be left in tears.
So, coming soon in your home town, is this feature presentation.
Awake from your slumber; prepare yourself for this epic compilation.
It is the "End of Time" you have been warned.
They'll be no further delay.
The Author says, "The stage is set, is your heart ready, the cameras roll today."

A Memory Of A Grandpa

Sparkling rainbow prisms dance across the dew-covered grass, bringing to memory your sparkling smile,
Filling me with comfort that promises me that life is indeed worthwhile.
Gentle and warm breezes embrace my body and soul,
Bringing to memory your presence upon this earth and making me miss you more than you'll ever know.
Intoxicating scents of freshly-turned gardening soil,
Bringing to memory your dedication to work your land and to hard work, which you remained most loyal.
The invading smell of freshly cut grass,
Bringing to memory your cow's sweet and delightful fragrant breath, making fond memories last.
Fluttering graceful wings enable the majestic butterfly,
Bringing to memory the softly swooping curtains of lashes that framed your glittering and passionate blue eyes.
Brilliant shining rays of the radiance of the sunshine,
Bringing to memory the loving touch within your warm embrace that was always pulsating through your open arms for me to find.
Magical tinkling of the whimsical wind chimes,
Bringing to memory delightful and sweet melodies of your laughter and endless memories of all of our good times.

Amanda Perry

The happiness of a bird's beautiful summer song,
Bringing to memory gay uplifting tones of musical whistles that to your lips did belong.
Sparkling and twinkling radiant dances of millions of fireflies,
Bringing to memory glorifying light from our Father above, which inside your soul brightly shines and never dies.
A crickets quiet serenade,
Bringing to memory peaceful and serene expressions upon your face as into nightly slumber you would gently fade.
Striking colors of red, orange, and yellow light up the sky at dawn's early break,
Bringing to memory the early hour in which you did always wake.
The horse, an animal of the most majestic beauty,
Bringing to memory joyous rides and a passion born deep within you; to care for these creatures, for you, was your love and your life, not just for you a mere duty.
The tantalizing aroma of buttery popcorn popping,
Bringing to memory evenings spent together in your reclining comfy chair, while on television a football game intensely watching.
Each changing season,
Bringing to memory fond and terrifying memories that seem to haunt my dreams for some reason.
The season of fall
For me is bittersweet. I love the brilliant changing colors of the tree's leaves and the crispness in the air, but fall is also the season that haunts me most of all…

Chasms And Bridges Within The Heart

The sight of a man in uniform, a policeman,
Bringing to memory that cold fall morning when a knock was heard on the door; to be able to ever forget, I don't think that I ever can.
Turning the world upside down,
Bringing to memory feelings of suffocation as if in a powerful current of the ocean's waves a destiny to drown.
Sounds of mournful weeping,
Bringing to memory a little girl lost and confused, missing your presence, which daily was she seeking.
The sight of cool and refreshing alcohol,
Bringing to memory the intoxicated driver who took a husband, a father, a grandfather, a friend, and one of the world's most greatest men from us all.
Warm, kind, and loving embraces,
Bringing to memory hearts broken and shattered in a million different places.
Cold winds and pouring drops of rain,
Bringing to memory the view atop the hill where I watched as they placed you into the freezing ground; rain, which was actually the angel's tears washing away the pain.
Dead and dying leaves falling from trees,
Bringing to memory depression as before tear-filled eyes all happiness suddenly flees.
Trees now lifeless, bare, and naked,
Bringing to memory a great loss of life most divinely sacred.
The silence of lonely nights,
Bringing to memory visions and nightmares full and thriving with endless frights.

Amanda Perry

Laughter a grandpa's voice are sounds slowly fading.
A photo and some reminiscing stories are all I have left of you remaining.
Year after year continues to pass on by.
Pain lessens and life continues on, but your memory never ever fades. I truly believe that you're looking down on us from your home up in the sky.
Promises from the Bible, from the Book, from Heaven
Let me know I'm okay and that we'll be together again; for me, these promises are one of God's greatest blessings.
Majestic and pure white billowing wings-
I know that you are one of God's most beautiful angels, and thinking of this vision joyously makes my heart sing.
A place without hate, murder, blood, and pain,
A place always full of love, life, untold beauty, and freedom became your eternal home, letting me know that death is definitely worth the gain.
Walking side by side right along with Jesus is how I see you now.
A face full of love, compassion, and finally peace as before your Father you joyously bow.
A life here on earth you spent working every day.
Now you are well-rested and with the children in Heaven you have time to play.
Surrounded by rolling and thriving open fields,
I can see you riding and caring for the majestic horses of Heaven; and to comfort and happiness my weary soul yields.
I miss you each and every day,
But I believe God called your name and needed you in a very special way.
I thank the Lord for the times we had together,
And I pray and patiently wait for the day that in Heaven you and I will live happily forever…

Chasms And Bridges Within The Heart

When I was in the second grade, my grandpa, Eugene Thomas Perry, was killed by a drunk driver in a car accident. They said he was going well over one hundred when he came off the exit of the interstate. He ran a red light, and the person he hit was my grandpa...

I was very young and didn't completely understand what had happened. I knew that he was never coming back, that he was gone forever, and that there was nothing that I or my family could do to save him. The hardest thing for me, then, was walking up to the open casket holding tightly onto my Aunt Theresa's hand. I knew that that was to be the last time I'd ever see papaw Gene on earth again...

I know that he is in Heaven and that he watches over us day by day. Sometimes, I can even sense his presence is here with us. He was a great man, my papaw, and a loving husband, father, and grandfather. He was the man that raised me; he was like my father. I miss him so much and I pray that I have made him proud. I long for that day when I can meet him in Heaven and see his beautiful face and wrap my arms around him...

But, until then, I will continue to remember him through my memories and photos and stories...

Papaw, I love you so much. I miss you more and more. I want to thank you for being my guardian angel and for watching over your family with each and every passing day. I hope that I have made you proud and that I will continue to do just that. How I wish you could be here to see Serenity. I know she would adore and love you. One day and one day very soon, we will all be together again. I cannot wait until that day! I will never stop thinking about you, and I will never stop loving you. You are in my heart and mind, always.

Amanda Perry

Psalm Of The King Of Glory

The earth is the Lord's, and the fullness thereof: the world, and they that dwell therein.
For He hath founded it upon the seas and established it upon the floods.
(Psalm 24:1-2)

My heart swells with tremendous appreciation and, with every beat, my blood flows only by God's amazing grace.
Standing in awestruck wonder, to the King of Glory, endless praises flow freely from lips which of His Glory does taste.
My face is lifted rapturously to the white splendor above;
Splendor of a wide-spreading apple-tree, overhead exploding a canopy of snowy fragrant bloom, a divine pleasure made from the King's everlasting eternal love.
Below the boughs, the air is full of a purple twilight.
A glimpse of painted sunset sky shines like a great rose window at the end of a cathedral's aisle; a perfect and peaceful calm engulfs the approaching night.
A stream nearby sparkles with a glory of many-shifting hues, the most spiritual shadings of rose and ethereal green, with other elusive tintings for which no name has ever been found.

Chasms And Bridges Within The Heart

The stream runs up into fringing groves of fir and maple and lays all darkly-translucent in their wavering shadows falling upon the ground.
A clear and mournfully-sweet chorus of many frogs begin a beautiful serenade,
Praising and worshipping the King of Glory for all that He has made…
In the darkness of the night and in the light of day,
The entire earth and its inhabitants recognize their Creator and to the King of Glory give praises in every imaginable way…
A huge cherry tree so thick-set with blossoms that hardly a green leaf can be seen,
Showers white blossoms down upon the earth's lushly-growing grass painted beautiful shades of green.
In a garden thriving with life, purple flowers blanket lilac trees,
Their dizzily sweet fragrance drifting upon the gentle whispers of the breeze.
Below the garden, a green field lush with clover
Flourishes and thrives from the most gentle and loving care given by its Heavenly Sower.
My beauty-loving eyes linger on it all.
My heart and soul to the King of Glory joyously does call.
Inhaling fragrances swirling upon the wind,
Heaven here on earth the King of Glory does willingly send.
I smile at the endless beauty all around me.
The air isn't just full of light… it is light, just as inspiring as it can be.

Amanda Perry

Unsuspecting tintings glimmer in the dark demesnes of the woods and glows in their alluring by-ways.
The spring sunshine sifts through the young green leaves, gently caressing each one with comforting warm rays.
Gay and merry trills of song can be heard praising the King of Glory most bold,
Leading the way to little hollows where a person feels as if they are bathing in a pool of liquid gold.
Fresh spring scents wafting up to Heaven… spice ferns… fir balsam… the whole some odor of newly-ploughed fields.
My heart leaps at the joy and radiance that this earth proudly yields.
Under the trees are wondrous star flowers.
Sheets of curly ferns blanket the earth, protecting it from harsh elements during all hours.
A babbling brook, white with strawberry blossoms and blue with violets and green with baby ferns,
Whispers quietly to my soul, and together for the King of Glory we delightfully yearn.
The earth rejoices in beautiful Heaven-sent bliss.
Radiant milky white peonies with the blood-red flecks at their hearts suddenly grab my attention, appearing as if bestowed upon each petal from God a most precious kiss.
I lift my eyes back up to the dazzling blue sky- so peaceful, so unchanged, so brilliantly blue.
I whisper praises to the King of Glory for saving my soul and opening my eyes up to see the majestic beauty of the new…

Chasms And Bridges Within The Heart

The Lord reigneth: let the earth rejoice; let the multitude of isles be glad thereof.
Clouds and darkness are round about him: righteousness and judgment are the habitation of his throne.
A fire goeth before him, and burneth up his enemies round about.
His lightnings enlightened the world: the earth saw and trembled.
The hills melted like wax at the presence of the Lord, at the presence of the Lord of the whole earth.
The heavens declare his righteousness, and all the people see his glory.
Confounded be all they that serve graven images, that boast themselves of idols: worship him, all ye gods.
Zion heard, and was glad; and the daughters of Judah rejoiced because of thy judgments, O Lord.
For thou, Lord, art high above all the earth: thou art exalted far above all gods.
Ye that love the Lord, hate evil: he preserveth the souls of his saints; he delivereth them out of the hand of the wicked.
Light is sown for the righteous, and gladness for the upright in heart.
Rejoice in the Lord, ye righteous; and give thanks at the remembrance of his holiness.
(Psalm 97:1-12)

Amanda Perry

Whom Shall I Send?

Through sheer glittering of a brilliant rainbow,
Past the brightness of the sun and its radiant glow…
A flight through the vastness of outer space,
Past the dazzlement of billions of twinkling stars lies the most divine and glorious place…
A great gate sparkling of the purest gold
Opens to reveal a sight most precious and glorious to behold…
Here, everything is alive and thriving with brilliant dew drops of radiant color;
Breathtaking colors that for the people on earth are not able to ever discover…
Grass so green and lushly soft as walking on clouds,
Beautiful liquid-clear songs of nature are the most welcoming sounds…
Along the bank of a gentle flowing river
Stands a mighty line of Willow trees, the wondrous peace givers…
The riverbed glitters with abundant diamonds and precious jewels,
Sharing immense beauty with the King who in this place righteously rules…
Here, flowers thrive with life and are always in bloom.
The Son always shines, for there is no need of darkness or the light of the stars or moon…

Chasms And Bridges Within The Heart

Tantalizing fragrances awaken all senses and make you feel alive,
Nurturing the soul, making it lift up to the bluest of skies and joyfully glide…
A chorus of angelic voices begin passionate exultations.
The Son shines even brighter as the Angels sing triumphant jubilations…
A throne of gold stands tall upon pure white billowing clouds.
A sheer curtain of tiny diamonds sparkle and all around the throne embracing it shrouds…
A bright light gently caresses each tiny diamond and radiates glorious rainbow prism bursts of light.
Every Angel bows, worshipping upon their knees at this miraculous and Holy sight…
A peaceful silence calms this entire place.
Endless love falls down like drops of rain from His Amazing Grace…
A mighty and clear amplified voice rings out from behind the sparkling curtain.
No man or being can possess such a voice; this voice is the voice of God, of that it is certain…
Strong and firm but also soft and gentle sounds the voice,
Saturating all with love and tremendous peace; to bow down and worship freely is the most gracious choice…
"Whom shall I send? Who will go for Me…"
"To the ends of the earth, who will rise up for their King…"
The Son pulsated with blinding beams of light,
The sound of His voice echoed, and His words caused tears to blur the Angels' sight…
"Here am I, send Me…"
"Here am I, Father, send Me…"

Amanda Perry

God sent His only Son down upon the earth.
He taught the people about Salvation and provided them with doctrine that enabled and also quenched spiritual thirst…
In the Holy name of His Father, He performed miracles and many people He healed.
Many people followed and believed in Him, in the Book of Life their names are and forever will be sealed…
His teachings provided hope of a new and better life,
But many people also rejected Him. Their hatred seared through their own heart; consuming and slicing like a knife…
He was betrayed and secretly arrested.
By Satan himself, His faith was viciously tested…
Blood poured in torrents down His battered body and formed great pools at His feet.
The soldiers laughed at His silence and each time His skin was ripped open as Jesus Christ they mercilessly beat…
A crown of thorns they pierced upon the skin of His head.
A massive cross they commanded Him to carry as to Golgotha He was led…
Nails pierced through precious hands and feet.
Soon, again, His Father in Heaven He would meet…
Jesus died willingly for you and I,
So that we could live forever and never burning die…
He brought to earth the gift of Salvation.
That, my friends, is a worthy Proclamation…
Generations and ages pass,
But the gift of life, Salvation, continues to thrive and to last…

Chasms And Bridges Within The Heart

Satan can and will not yet be tamed.
He forcefully releases his fiery power, devouring the earth and many people in burning flames…
Families torn apart by his hatred;
His goal and main mission is to destroy everything that is Holy and sacred…
Isis, a powerful and massive group of followers, he has created and collected.
Taking over the world, Satan's earthly empire they have erected…
A young man, covered completely in raiment of black,
Fearfully prepares for the next massacre of brutal attack…
He wonders if there is a better way as he dutifully sharpens his knife.
He wonders if bloodshed and violence is the true meaning of a person's life…
God looks down upon the earth.
He knows that truth and redemption is what this young man's soul does thirst…
"Whom shall I send? Who will go for Me…"
"To the ends of the earth, who will rise up for their King…"
A woman, broken and battered,
Stares at her bruised reflection and wonders if her life really matters…
Never was she shown kindness or love.
Never taught the love of God, she takes her last breath as she slides under the water in the bathtub…
"Whom shall I send? Who will go for Me…"
"To the ends of the earth, who will rise up for their King…"

Amanda Perry

An officer, blinded by the color of someone's skin,
Finds himself consumed by intense hatred and searches for a victim whose life he can end…
He doesn't realize the hurt and chaos he can make.
He doesn't even consider the other path that he can take…
"Whom shall I send? Who will go for Me…"
"To the ends of the earth, who will rise up for their King…"
A country on the other side of the earth crumbles from a massive earthquake.
People are lost in the rubble, multiple diseases quickly outbreak, there's no food and no clean water; the surviving people wonder exactly how much more suffering they can take…
"Whom shall I send? Who will go for Me…"
"To the ends of the earth, who will rise up for their King…"
America is no longer the Land of the Free.
A nation fallen away from the foundation that her Father's built based entirely on God; her eyes have been gouged out and hope no longer can she see…
The symbol of freedom, the American Flag now causes controversy and is a great offense.
The name of God is banned from schools and so is prayer; Satan and his army are viciously conquering and their grip on America they will not relent…
"Whom shall I send? Who will go for Me…"
"To the ends of the earth, who will rise up for their King…"

Chasms And Bridges Within The Heart

We as Christians need to rise up together.
We share a bond with Jesus that absolutely no one can sever...
"Who will stand and fight? Who will come with me..."
"To the ends of the earth, who will rise up for their King..."
"Here am I, send me..."
"Here am I, Lord, please send me..."
A world fallen from Grace,
Lord, I know I'm not alone in seeking Your face...

I pray for the wisdom.
I pray for the strength.
I praise You for this poetical vision.
I pray that the names in Your Book of Life from reading this poem grows immensely in length...
I praise You for accepting me and wiping away all of my stains.
I pray for the application of my trembling voice.
I pray for the people of this world to take the time to listen to the silence, instead of the worldly noise...
I pray for the Christians in this world, that they remain strong and steadfast in their faith, that they realize that outside the walls of their church people need their witness now more than ever, and that they remember what Salvation is truly about.
Lord, I can only pray that of this movement I will be partaking...
I pray for Isis that they can learn about You and want to change their ways.
I pray they find the shelter under Your wings and there will forever want to stay.

Amanda Perry

For God so loved the world, that He gave His only begotten Son, that whosoever believeth on Him should not perish, but have everlasting life.
(John 3:16)

Jesus died for everybody: you, me, addicts, members of Isis- He loves everyone and wants everyone to inherit the Kingdom of Heaven. We are to pray for our enemies and show them love; treat them as fellow brethren…

"Whom shall I send? Who will go for Me…"
"To the ends of the earth, who will rise up for their King…"
"Lord, You shall send me, I will go for You…"
"To the ends of the earth, I will rise up for my King…"
"Here am I, send me…"
"Here am I, Lord, send me…"

Chasms And Bridges Within The Heart

A Wedding Eternal

A body, once broken, finds eternal healing in a most glorious and righteous flow.
Satin-soft ribbons of purest white caress and envelop a once-lost and shattered soul, bringing to life the most softly radiant glow.
Born upon gentle breezes, calming and peaceful whispers trace cooling promises of euphoric bliss upon human skin.
Memories of regret and intense pain are forever washed away; into the river of the darkness of the past these memories dwindling do blend.
Mystic white roses enveloped by softly scented baby's breath surround a breathtaking blood red rose.
A wedding bouquet symbolizing Christ's pure life and the death that for this bride He willingly chose.
Covering an awakening soul is a dazzling diamond-filled mist: the bride's long flowing veil.
Trembling from sensational warmth and pulsating love, the bride releases her whole life: past, present, and future; the veil is pulled away and at that same exact moment, the bride feels her chains being broken from her eternal Hell.

Amanda Perry

Heaven's flood gates suddenly open, and showers of cleansing and purifying streams of healing engulf the uplifted soul.
Rapturous rainbow ribbons of Christ's eternal love fall upon the bride's body and continuously does roll.
Like a rose blooming into newfound life, rapturous joy and endless happiness blooms inside a newly-beating heart.
Sparkling tears fall from thankful and uplifted eyes as the bride praises and worships Christ for this amazing and glorious new start.
Locked doors within the heart are suddenly splintered and reopened.
The bride finds her lost abilities of passionately dreaming and hoping.
Gentle yet intoxicating fragrances ignite the senses with the splendor of eternal wedded bliss.
The bride surrenders her life over and accepts the gentle purity of Christ's long-awaited kiss….
Tingling sensations flow through her veins.
Her heart beats anew as her mind realizes that purity, cleanliness, and everlasting love she has miraculously gained.
Burdens and shadows of her past are quickly from her shoulders lifted.
The world she knew appears entirely different as if by some collision in space it has been left tilted.
Her hands are covered with warm and glowing hands, which bring great comfort in this earthly place.
Her eyes fill with grateful tears as they gaze upon the two deep, bloodstained scars within these glowing hands; love and devotion pulsate throughout her soul as she acknowledges and accepts His Amazing Grace.

Chasms And Bridges Within The Heart

A weightless soul brought from the darkness and chains of Hell
Radiates the brightest of lights and yearning for Heaven under the wings of Christ does now dwell.
A chorus of Angels sing praises so immensely sweet.
The first wedding dance has begun; the dance floor, billowing and soft, are clouds beneath her feet.
Long-suppressed laughter bubbles up from deep within.
Having forgot her own laughter's sound, she surprises herself and joyously does grin.
Gaining freedom….
Gaining an eternal entrance into Christ's beloved Kingdom…
Gaining back her soul which was deeply lost…
Gaining love and life which long ago, for her, Christ paid the cost…
Gaining trust, once again…
Gaining a Father, Brother, Lover, and Best Friend…
Gaining faith…
Gaining acceptance in the beautiful masterpiece of her being that God has masterfully made…
Gaining a new and clean life…
Gaining a companion who will hold her hands all through life's struggles and strife…
Gaining her destiny…
That will one day lead her to her home in all eternity…

Amanda Perry

Therefore if any man be in Christ, he is a new creature: old things are passed away; behold, all things are become new.
And all things are of God, who hath reconciled us to himself by Jesus Christ, and hath given to us the ministry of reconciliation;
(2 Corinthians 5:17-18)

Lord, I ask Your forgiveness of my sins. Help me to forgive myself. You see the deepest parts of my heart. You know my guilt. You know my regret. I want to be able to stand clean before Your presence. I want to live life without fear. I accept Your Healing. Thank You for changing my blood-red sins into a blanket of snow-white purity. Thank You for the realization that I had to give myself away to You completely in order to move on in my life.
Thank You, Lord, for taking my sins to the cross.
In Your merciful name,
Amen…

Chasms And Bridges Within The Heart

If The Lord Is With Us, Who Can Come Against Us?

Beneath my feet, the earth violently quakes and trembles.
The enemies are coming, marching steadily in unison and waving their flags as signs of horrific death symbols.
The shackles and chains of death surround me.
The floods of chaotic destruction sweep over me and, suddenly, I can't breathe.
The grave opens up and, taunting, it calls me to my final resting place.
The darkness of death reaches out and caresses my face.
The foundations of the majestic and beautiful mountains begin to shake.
Freedom… my freedom they are coming to take.
Nauseating aromas of death and smoke envelop them.
The Devil marches before them, promising them great victory in the end.
Smoke continuously pours from nostrils flared.
Glowing coals flame within their eyes as at their victims they forcefully stare.
Devouring flames leap from sin-covered lips.
O, Angel of Death, have you truly come to deliver your fateful kiss?

Amanda Perry

They thunder from the open gates of Hell,
Now released among my nation to freely dwell.
Above my country, dark storm clouds fill the sky.
They chant in unison: "All Christians are to suffer and die!"
Warnings and threats soar upon the wings of the wind.
It has arrived: The Beginning of the End…
They are covered in the Devil's darkness, veiling their approach with dense storm clouds.
They thrive on bloodshed and celebrate with their victims' tortured and pain-filled howls…
Suddenly, the heavens open, and a brilliant and fearful light breaks through the clouds.
The Lord thunders from Heaven, and the brilliance of His presence falls around His children and protectively shrouds.
Raining down from the open sky falls hail and great burning coals.
Panic-driven people fall to their knees and begin praying for their very souls.
Great flashes of lighting strike at the trembling ground.
Monstrous booms of thunder over the whole world is the only detectable sound.
The enemies are confused, and frightfully they run scattered.
Their leader is now nowhere to be seen, and all of their plans and duties have been shattered…

Chasms And Bridges Within The Heart

O, how I love You, Lord; You are my Strength.
For You, I will go any distance and conquer any length.
The Lord is my Savior, my Fortress, and my Rock.
He holds the only key to my heart's eternal lock.
He is my Shield, the Strength of my Salvation, and my Stronghold.
I will call on the Lord, who is worthy of praise, for His mighty works are wondrous to behold.
He has reached down from Heaven and has rescued me.
He has delivered me from my powerful enemies.
From those who hate me and are too strong for me,
Who attack me at a moment when I am the weakest, the Lord upholds me.
To a place of safety and peace, He leads me.
He has rescued me because He delights in me.
The Lord rewards those who do right.
Keep the ways of the Lord and in His embrace He will hold you tight.
I will not turn from my God to follow evil.
For me, that thought will never even be conceivable.
The Lord will reward me for doing right,
Because of the innocence of my hands in His sight.
To the faithful, You show Yourself faithful.
I stand in awe at the miracles of which from You are capable.
To the pure, You show Yourself pure,
Of Your love and Grace, I am most sure.
Lord, You have brought light to my life.
For You and Your gift of Salvation, I will gladly fight.
My God, You light up my darkness and radiantly shine.
I am Yours and, Lord, You are mine…

Amanda Perry

As for God, His way is perfect and real.
For all of those looking to Him for protection, He is an indestructible shield.
For who is God except the Lord?
Into my broken body, His Spirit continuously does pour.
Who but our God is a solid rock?
He is the safe harbour for His growing flock.
He has given me the shield of His great Salvation.
My soul radiates His glow of life and love and bursts with elation.
His right hand supports me.
His glory enables me to fully see.
The Lord lives!!!
Victory and life eternal He faithfully gives!!!
He is the God who subdues the nations under the Heavens.
He rescues you from your enemies with His majesty and glory as weapons.
He holds me safe beyond the reach of the Devil's army.
He saves me from violent opponents who are out to harm me.
For this, O Lord, I will praise You among the nations.
I will sing joyfully to Your name and praise You with endless exultations!
For, Lord, if You are with me,
Who can come against me?

Chasms And Bridges Within The Heart

Nothing That We Can't Handle

The world today is crazy and full of hatred, murder, revenge, and bloodshed; depression and worry quickly set in, but no matter what distressing times that I face... when pouring rain and violent storms replace the sunny weather... when things that I counted on fail to sustain me, I rest in the comfort that there's nothing we can't handle, Lord, together.

If the people whom I thought were friends and family begin to act more like foes... if I begin to lose the precious things that to my heart I hold most dear, I know that always I can tell it all to You; You are always here to guide me, and Your ears are always open for my voice to hear.

When the earthly world around me crumbles and dissolves right before my very own eyes... when problems and secrets seem way to great for me to upon my shoulders bear, You will always be there for me, Lord, I know; I can come to You with folded hands and bow on bended knees in prayer.

It's such a comfort for me, Lord, to finally realize that You will always be my King, my Lord, my Savior; to forever share my burdens, my worries, and my cares. You will forever accept and endlessly love me and will always support me to the very end...

Amanda Perry

At The Foot Of The Cross

Gasping for air, I can't breathe, drowning in my own shame and sorrow.
Dreams and ambitions disappear as I realize that there is no promise or hope of tomorrow.
Hanging my tormented head in utter defeat, while fearing that the battle is truly over and that I have already lost the war.
So tired of trying and always failing, this battle, I just cannot fight anymore...
I feel...
I feel...
I feel...
All balance fleeing as my mind and vision begins to endlessly reel.
Something comforting is suddenly reaching out to me,
Majestic and alluring; a beautiful cross becomes all I can see.
Deepening sadness seeps through to my pounding heart.
A man hanging upon the cross radiates a bright glow; saving me from the embrace of the dark.
His body is mangled and badly broken; blood flows in continuous streams.
Flesh torn violently open and apart expose broken and shattered bones; a vision which should haunt every sinner's dreams...

Chasms And Bridges Within The Heart

Cascading drops of blood falling to the ground are the only detectable sound.
Tears welling up in my eyes as I gaze at how His body, to the cross, is bound.
Each hand has been pierced with a nail,
His feet held together in the same manner, as well.
The aroma of blood drives me to my knees.
Dragging my battle-scarred body which is full of sin's accumulating disease.
Slowly and shakily, I crawl to the foot of the cross,
Sobbing...
Weeping...
"Please, Father, forgive me, but I tried. I tried so hard, and still I have lost..."
Growing very still and silent is the air all around me.
A comforting peace falls upon me, enabling me to fully breathe.
I hear His voice as clear as the approaching dawn,
"My child, though you are tired and weary,
You cannot stop, you must go on...
You just can't stop. I will give you strength to go on."
At the foot of the cross where I met Him,
I felt myself heal as I confessed my burdens and sins...
At the foot of the cross where He died,
Salvation and Redemption for me He did provide.
I felt love as I knelt there in His presence...
He is the reason for life's very existence.

Amanda Perry

I felt hope as I looked into those beautiful eyes…
He gathered me to Him, and under His wings I shall now and forever abide.
All around us, God's light clearly shone.
Together we marched through my lifetime to heal every wound I had ever known.
I found bits of my dreams long-forgotten and pieces of my life on the floor.
I watched as He tenderly blessed them and my life was worth living, once more.
I knew then why this war I had been losing.
At the foot of the cross came the choice I should have been choosing.
I knew also why I had not grown.
I had been fighting the battle all alone…
I had been fighting my battle all alone.
At the foot of the cross where I met Him,
At the foot of the cross where He died for my sin.
Immediately, I knew that together we could meet any challenge…
Together… just my Lord and I.
Together… just my Lord Jesus and I…

Chasms And Bridges Within The Heart

Admirable Devotion

A personality enveloped by happiness and bliss.
An unbreakable bond long-developed before the first precious kiss.
Assuming a role that you did not have to play,
Showering fatherly affections; a very sacred and special part in my heart you will forever stay.
Dazzling like diamonds is a most beautiful smile.
At a very young age, it was you who taught me that life is indeed worthwhile.
Always accepting of me, like a daughter of your very own.
With you in my life, I have never or ever will feel hopeless and alone.
Ribbons of love swirling within your embrace,
In your hugs, I always find a most welcoming and calming place.
Sparkling blue windows open to a most glorious soul,
Its light cannot be diminished; it radiates outward and sets your entire being aglow.
The simple things in life you taught me to appreciate.
The sound of gently rolling waves of a river, the warmth and togetherness of a crackling campfire, the ecstatic thrill of that first tug on a fishing line are all things you gave to me that within my memories and soul still continue to thrive and to saturate.

Amanda Perry

A heart that beats to share love and help to all that need.
In many lives God has allowed you to touch and to plant your nurturing seed.
Hands that have done hard work and know endless strife;
These same hands bring tremendous comfort and healing to my very existence in life.
Laughter that brings smiles and happiness to all who have the pleasure to hear.
A sense of humor and personality that has the amazing ability to draw all people near.
Fatherly wisdom and guidance you freely pass unto me.
Without you in my life, I just honestly don't know who or where I would be.
Many situations you have helped me through and have been there for me through them all,
Building up my confidence and helping me to remain standing firm and tall.
Such an immense impact in my life you have made.
I thank God everyday for not taking you away, for letting you on this earth continue to stay.
The only one person worthy of my admiration
Is my uncle for whom I have deep regard and tremendous appreciation.
The only figure in my life who is irreplaceable
Is my Uncle Larry to me…
Who is and always will be very special…

Happy Birthday,
I love you more than words can ever describe!
Amanda

About The Author

Amanda Perry grew up in the beautiful state of West Virginia. She first began writing when she was in the second grade, after her grandfather was killed in a terrible car accident. It wasn't until she reached her mid-twenties, though, that she began writing about her experiences in her life. She had always wanted to help people, and she realized that by sharing her writing, she could do just that.

What inspires Amanda to write is her faith in God and her journey as she passes through this life. Her writing is all based on real experiences and what God has laid on her heart to share with the readers.

Amanda is the very proud mother of one very beautiful five-year-old little girl whom she named Serenity Leigh. Her daughter inspires all that she does and brings her permanent joy and light in this ever-darkening world. Amanda adores being a mother and thanks God every day for her growing daughter. Amanda uses her writing to draw closer to the Lord, that through her work she might worship and praise Jesus Christ for all He has done and is doing in her life.

Acknowledgements

First, I would like to thank the Lord for blessing my mind and my hand in writing. I used to dream of one day becoming a writer, but I never thought that my dream would ever come true. God spoke to me and led me to write about my life and my experiences. Maybe, there are people out there who are going through similar things that I have been through and have written about. I pray that God uses my writing to reach out to those people and to encourage them.

A huge thank you goes out to:

My grandma and mom, Lytia and Lisa, for a lifetime of love and continuous support, for still holding my hand through the journey of life, and for never ever giving up on me.

My daughter, Serenity, for showing me the meaning of life and for blessing me with unconditional love, never-ending happiness, and tremendous strength.

My very talented and close friend, Bathsheba Daily, for providing me with this wonderful opportunity and for giving me that "nudge" that I needed to get started.

My friends at True Beginnings Publishing.

Scott Thomas Myers, a brilliant poet and writer who took the time to read my writing and who believed in my talent and urged me to never stop writing.

Selina Ahnert, a very beautiful and talented woman who stayed up many nights helping to bring this book together. Tremendous thanks also goes to her for the amazing cover of this book.

Mountain State Christian School, my highschool, for planting the seed of Christianity in my life and soul and for providing me with knowledge and understanding of God and His Holy Word.

My biological father, Joe Sovine, for reading my poems and for giving me positive feedback that gave me the courage to keep writing.

A very close friend who I also consider my mom, Tina Markham Burroughs, for her encouraging words and her belief and faith in me. She has helped me overcome so many obstacles and has helped me to remain strong in my faith.

My other "papaw," Kenneth Markham, for showing me the love of a grandpa and for always being there for me when I needed advice, love, and comfort. A great man of God that has left such a wondrous impression in my life.

My other "mamaw," Eunice Markham, for showering me always with love and acceptance and for sharing her love of God and knowledge of the Bible with me.

Steve Burroughs, for his words of wisdom and comfort over the past years and for his gentle spirit, sense of humor, and strong-standing faith and wisdom in God.

My beautiful sister, Megan Perry Martin, for always being there for me and believing in me.

Retta Nelson, who is like a sister to me, for always accepting and loving me and for being there when I always needed her.

My best friend, Mary Nelson Parsons, and her amazing family, for always being there and for always accepting my craziness. Thank you, Mary, for teaching me to stand up for myself and to always remain strong, no matter what I'm facing.

My online family and friends for their support and advice.

www.ingramcontent.com/pod-product-compliance
Lightning Source LLC
LaVergne TN
LVHW041249080426
835510LV00009B/659